D0427305

PRAISE FOR JOHANNA STEIN

"Johanna Stein is lovely, insightful, and a big bowl of funny."

—JEFF GARLIN, comedian/writer/producer, *Curb Your Enthusiasm, The Goldbergs*

"Johanna Stein has a way of taking the good, the bad, and the ugly and turning it into a delicious piece of candy. ('Mind candy' of course, as real candy is 'bad' for you as any good mother knows). Simply put: I love her writing. I love the way she lays it all out there with such honesty and candor and tremendous relatability."

—MO COLLINS, actress and comedian, *MADtv, Parks and Recreation*

"Johanna Stein's wit, humor, compassion, and quirky underdog view on life make her stories a pure joy to read. I just cannot get enough of her writing."

—TRACY VILAR, actress, *House M.D.*

"Since her days as a comic with a guitar, writer/comedienne Johanna Stein has never failed to surprise, delight, and blow audiences away with her fearless storytelling. And when I say fearless, I don't mean the, 'Gee, sometimes my kids make me so mad I want to have two glasses of chardonnay!' kind. No, I mean fearless in the making you gasp, 'Oh sh*t she did not do that!' way. Stein is the kind of writer we all aspire to be, the fab girl next door who lures you in with unadorned honesty and witty prose and then slams you in to the messy truth in such a viscerally compelling way that you cannot not be moved to laughter, to tears, and most of all to appreciating the great joy of what it means to be human."

—DANI KLEIN MODISETT, writer/producer/editor, *Afterbirth*, *Huffington Post* contributor

How Not to
Calm a Child
on a Plane

HOW NOT TO
CALM A CHILD
ON A PLANE

And Other Lessons in Parenting
from a Highly Questionable Source

JOHANNA STEIN

Da Capo
LIFE
LONG

A Member of the Perseus Books Group

Copyright © 2014 by Johanna Stein

All rights reserved. No part of this publication may be reproduced,
stored in a retrieval system, or transmitted, in any form or by any
means, electronic, mechanical, photocopying, recording, or otherwise,
without the prior written permission of the publisher. Printed in the
United States of America. For information, address Da Capo
Press, 44 Farnsworth Street, 3rd Floor, Boston, MA 02210

Designed by Linda Mark
Set in 11.5 point ITC Esprit Std by the Perseus Books Group

Some of the essays in this book have appeared previously in slightly
different forms and/or with different titles in the following publications:
The New York Times Motherlode column: "How Not to Calm a Child on a
Plane" and "The Most Wonderful Time of the Year"; *Parents* magazine:
"A Pregnant Pause" and "One Is Enough"; *Afterbirth: Stories You Won't
Read in a Parenting Magazine* (St. Martin's Press): "Spoiled Milk."

Library of Congress Cataloging-in-Publication Data

Stein, Johanna.
  How not to calm a child on a plane : and other lessons in
parenting from a highly questionable source / Johanna Stein.
    pages cm
  ISBN 978-0-7382-1734-5 (hardback)—
  ISBN 978-0-7382-1735-2 (e-book) 1. Parenting—Humor.
  2. Child rearing—Humor. I. Title.
  HQ755.8.S7224 2014
  649'.1—dc23

                                        2013048709

First Da Capo Press edition 2014
ISBN: 978-0-7382-1374-5 (paperback)
ISBN: 978-0-7382-1375-2 (e-book)

Published by Da Capo Press
A Member of the Perseus Books Group
www.dacapopress.com

Note: The names and identifying details of people
associated with events described in this book have been
changed. Any similarity to actual persons is coincidental.

Da Capo Press books are available at special discounts for bulk purchases
in the U.S. by corporations, institutions, and other organizations. For more
information, please contact the Special Markets Department at the Perseus Books
Group, 2300 Chestnut Street, Suite 200, Philadelphia, PA, 19103, or call
(800) 810-4145, ext. 5000, or e-mail special.markets@perseusbooks.com.

10 9 8 7 6 5 4 3 2 1

For David and Sadie,
without whom my life would be empty
and so would this book

CONTENTS

A PREGNANT PAUSE

It's a gorgeous August day in Southern California, the kind that makes you think you've just stepped into a 1980s music video by the Go-Go's. I am at a beach barbecue, surrounded by people in skimpy swimsuits. This being Manhattan Beach, we're not talking Average Joes here; we're talking the most perfect human specimens ever to have evolved from an amoeba with six-pack abs. My usual response to finding myself in a place like this would be to pluck my eye out with a spoon and/or cut off my dangly bits with a steak knife. But not today, because today I am CWC: Chubby With Cause. Today I am six months pregnant.

Six months: the sweet spot. Big enough to show, but not so engorged that I feel like a billboard for *Alien 5:*

This Time It's Serious. The second trimester has been kind to me, and I am feeling all of the things the books say I should feel: powerful, feminine, and intuitive, if maybe a little gassy. But most of all, I am in a state of perpetual emotional ecstasy. I spend the majority of my waking moments thinking about, talking about, and fantasizing about my future perfect motherhood with my future perfect baby, and when I do it's always in soft-focus, with lots of drapey material, dappled sunlight, and James Taylor music. I feel so happy, I could puke a friggin rainbow.

I'm sitting at a picnic table with some friends—some single, non-incubating friends—when a woman in a bikini walks over and asks if she can borrow a bottle opener. She is friendly, attractive, and very fit, except for her very exposed tummy, which is taut yet full; there's no mistaking it, this is a belly full of arms and legs. Sizing up the bulge, I take her to be four, maybe five, months along. Then again, she's in such great shape, she may be deep into her third trimester. For all I know, she's fixing to squirt that kid out in the next ten minutes.

I smile and give her a knowing wink; she smiles and gives me a knowing wink back. You know that wink, the wink that is shared between Mac owners, Volkswagen drivers, Canadian tourists, and closeted gay rugby players. That wink that says, "Hey, you. . . . It's me! We're members of the same tribe! . . ." (in our case the pregnant-sister-goddess-life-givers tribe). ". . . And aren't we fan-friggin-precious-tastic?"

So we're smiling and winking and squinching and basking in our perfect pregnant goddess-ness, when finally I touch her hand and lean in to speak, but this time with actual words.

"How far along are you?" I ask.

She tilts her head, blinks, and says, "I'm not pregnant."

You might think that the force of my sphincter rising up into my throat would have rendered me speechless, but no, not so. In fact, before I can stop and take a moment to either (a) slam my head into the lifeguard stand or (b) throw myself into a smoldering barbecue pit, my mouth opens to let yet another ingenious question flop out:

"Oh!" I say. "So, did you just *have* a baby?"

Exactly like that.

"Did you just *have* a baby?"

With added guttural emphasis on the word "have."

"Did you just *HAVE* a baby??"

Bikini Lady looks so intensely into my eyes, so deeply into my being, that she makes contact with my dead ancestors and shames them for having contributed to my gene pool.

"No," she says. "I did not. Just. *HAVE*. A baby."

"Oh," I say and then feel a sharp pinch on my leg. It is one of my friends, who, in addition to having just welted me, is mentally recording this moment so that she can remind me of it on a monthly basis, apparently until the day that one of us dies. Her talonlike grip inflicts a bolt of pain that wakes me from my moron trance, at which point the verbal tripping begins: "I'm sorry, it's just that . . . you're so fit . . . and gorgeous . . . I just thought . . . you're so fit, except for the . . . you're just so gorgeous and fit!"

Bikini Lady says nothing. So in order to fill the awkward silence, I reach into myself and pull out the last tool left in my useless, rusting tool box: "I'm sorry, I don't know what I'm saying. *I'm drunk.*"

Bikini Lady looks at me like I have just sprouted a testicle on my face. She uses the bottle opener to crack the beer that was in her left hand all along,* then walks away, kicking up sand with her perfectly pedicured, unpregnant feet.

Now, I've done stupid things in my life, but nothing in recent memory that compares to the blatant douchebaggery of this moment. And, while I do believe that Bikini Lady led me on during our "we-are-the-pregnant-world" wink-a-thon, even a brainless jellyfish knows you never ask a lady if she is "with child," even if said child is bungee jumping on the end of an umbilical cord that's dangling from said lady's lady bits. But no, I couldn't even stop there; I had to travel the extra creepy mile of accusing her of having just birthed a baby, as if that were the only reasonable explanation for the remarkable potbelly on her otherwise perfect bod. For all I know, she has a tumor the size of a volleyball growing in there . . . Then again, maybe she just has weak abs; maybe she's eight weeks into a twelve-week workout regimen, and next week she's going to start working on her core. Or even worse, what if she is/was/is trying to get pregnant? Oh, God, I can't even go there . . . And then to try to skate out

---

*Because apparently, I'm not only insensitive but legally blind as well.

of it with the old "I'm a pregnant alcoholic" excuse? Wow. Now *I'm* embarrassed for my ancestors.

As I sit in the suddenly way-too-hot California sun, I take a moment to contemplate my grand mal faux pas. Just moments ago, I was basking in the glow-y image of myself as an intuitive, benevolent, patchouli-scented earth mother. And now—approximately eight minutes and one throbbing leg later—I'm a jackass who makes bad decisions, speaks without thinking, and has an annoying need to be right all the time.

In other words, I am still me, only fatter.

Now, several years later, I have grown strangely grateful for my beach-blanket blooper, and even though it causes me to sweat profusely just thinking about it, I am compelled to tell the story again and again to anyone who will listen. I think it's because that was the moment I realized that nothing about parenthood would conform to my expectations. Sure, pregnancy and parenthood may have changed me, but not in the hippiefied, wind-chimey ways I'd expected. I was no more intuitive, serene, or feminine as a pregnant person than I was before I reproduced. Other than being a few sizes larger, in the most essential "me" ways, I was still the same dopey "me" I'd always been. And most days, that's an oddly comforting thought—though probably not to a certain bikini-wearing lady with weak abs and bad posture, who just wanted to enjoy a cold beer on a hot day.

LIGHTS, CAMERA, PUSH!

It starts with the money shot.

No preamble, no intro, no warning. Just a high-res, point-blank shot of a pair of legs stretched to maximum capacity. Smack-dab in the middle of them, at the point of juncture, is the bulbous, misshapen knot of flesh that is responsible for the presence of every single person in this delivery room right now.

Yes, there is a birth video.

I recently had the opportunity to view said video,[*] the one that the husband made five years ago to commemorate the birth of our child.

---

[*]I accidentally clicked on it while searching my computer for a video of a penguin shoving another penguin into an ice hole. The screen grabs were eerily similar.

It took me a moment to understand what I was look-ing at—we'd never actually watched it, and when I finally did comprehend what it was, I called for my husband with the manly bellow that I reserve for occasions of such magnitude. He rushed into the room, because (a) he's a caring and responsive spouse and (b) he enjoys the sound of panic in my voice.

When he saw what was on my computer screen (and therefore on our afternoon agenda), he took a deep breath, looked down at the floor, and said, "Wow. Okay then. Let's do this."

⤳

We're not "those kinds" of people. We don't take roman-tic photos, gaze into each other's eyes, or leave loving notes around the house for the other to find. Not that we don't have those feelings—it's just that we're incapable of expressing them like most normal human beings.

We are, what you might call, "unemotional anti-romantics." Once, before we were married, the then boy-friend was freelancing in an ad agency office alongside a litter of hipster frat-boy types, and I refused to end a phone conversation with him until he told me that he loved me. After several minutes of cajoling, he gave in and whis-pered a sweet "I love you" into the phone, at which point I yelled, "YOU SAPPY BASTARD!" then hung up on him and cackled myself into a lengthy coughing fit. You may find this distasteful, and honestly I can't disagree. My behavior was deplorable—yet he would be the first to tell you it was the moment he realized that one day he would make me his bride. Such is the effed-uppitiness of our relationship.

And so this videotape—I'm not sure what made us think that filming the birth of our child was a good idea. In the first place, I can't stand having my photo taken, and that's at the best-haired-and-complexioned of times; I have one barely tolerable camera angle (15 degrees to the right of center, chin tucked, half-open-mouthed smile) that has taken me years to perfect, the result being that in most photos, I tend to look like a brain-injured wax version of myself. So why I thought that having a video camera trained on me, during a wildly uncontrollable medical procedure, from what is a terrible angle for anyone not starring in a porno flick . . . well, I really can't say. Another thing I really can't say is that there was an ulterior goal in the making of this birth video—i.e., that we hoped to show it to the child's first boyfriend on her prom night . . . or that we were planning to upload it to YouTube in hopes of my junk becoming the next v(ag)iral sensation. There was virtually no good reason to film it.

And still we filmed it.

And now, God help us, we are going to watch it.

～

"Using your mind it is possible to enter into a state of relaxation so complete that your delivery can not only be easy and enjoyable, it may even be a pleasurable experience."

That was what the hypnobirthing brochure promised.

Now, I am generally pretty suspicious of anything that smells even vaguely New Agey; I am so anti–New Age that just the sight of a man's naked feet in sandals makes me nauseous.

And then there was the obvious question: did we *need* a birthing class? Does anyone, really, considering that birth is the single most common act of the mammalian species, next to dying, taxes, and seeing the musical *Jersey Boys*? It was going to happen whether or not we attended a five-week, $250 hippie fest fifteen miles from our home, right?

On the other hand, I am a big believer in formal education; I'd take a workshop in armpit farting if I thought it would improve my technique enough to include it on a résumé.

But the real reason I signed us up is that when it comes to hypnosis, I am, what you might call, the ideal candidate.

When I was in junior high, our school was visited by a mentalist-hypnotist known as "Reveen!" who performed his entire routine for three hundred seventh and eighth graders just before lunch. Although it didn't carry the titillating potential of a Friday-night dance-and-heavy-pet-athon, the event was exciting enough to draw a full-house crowd (if you don't count the twenty or so kids who sneaked out to the basketball court to get high).

When Reveen! took the stage and asked for volunteers, I threw my hand into the air and stormed the stage. That's how I became a featured player in Reveen!'s "stage hypnosis act." I was later told that during the forty-five-minute presentation, I shouted "BOCK BOCK!" and laid a nest-ful of (mime) eggs, I played a (mime) drum solo during the biggest rock show in history, I (mime) canoed across a gator-filled river, and when Reveen! directed me to leap into the (actual) arms of the nearest male teacher and hug him as though he was my long-lost love, that's what I did.

I don't know exactly how or why his techniques worked, but the fact is that I was clearly "suggestive" to this portly, jet-black-toupeed man, on what amounts to pretty thin grounds (i.e., my desire to help him entertain a mob of pre-pubescent teens in a gymnasium that smelled like feet).*

Now that I actually have a good reason for undergoing hypnosis—i.e., I am preparing to pass a pumpkin through the eye of a needle (and a flappy one at that)—I believe that my suggestibility will be stronger than ever.

↜↝

With six weeks to go until D(ue) Day, the husband and I took our spots on a carpeted classroom floor with five other couples in various stages along the pregnancy con-tinuum. We went around the room introducing ourselves, and it didn't take long for the husband and me to realize that we were surrounded on all sides by people who use words like *Empowerment, Nurturing,* and *Sacred Space,* and say them frequently and often with closed eyes and weird, serene smiles.

---

*Also, if I'm being totally honest, I'm pretty sure I went along with the whole thing just to impress that one guy in English class who could re-ally work a pair of Hammer pants. Though why I thought that shuffling across the stage like a chicken would impress a thirteen-year-old guy—your guess is as good as mine.

After a few minutes, a woman floated into the room, dressed in a flowing muumuu-esque outfit that had no clear beginning or end. This was our instructor, Linneah, and as she pulled out a bunch of sage and then set it on fire, wafting the smoke around the room "to remove the negative energies and unwanted spirits," for a moment I wondered if she was talking about us.

There were phrases to chant ("Innnn . . . Ouuuuut . . . Gentle waaaaaves of waaaaterrrrr") and breathing techniques to help "breathe your baby out of your vagina." There were videos to watch and diaries to keep. And there were relaxation tapes, voiced by Linneah herself, which we were instructed to listen to every night, despite the fact that Linneah's speaking voice sounded like Fran Drescher on tranquilizers.

And although the five-week course challenged every bone in my immature (SHE SAID "BONE!" HAW! HAW!) body, and every week I came down with a stress headache from struggling not to giggle every time Linneah spoke, lit incense, or cupped my cheek in her hand while recommending a brand of olive oil to rub on my perineum,* we persevered because we both felt that, considering we were about to be parents, it was important that we rise above our juvenile tendencies. Also, Linneah had a strict no-refunds policy.

During the fifth and final class, we learned that one of our classmates had gone into labor early. Linneah reported that, not only had she done it all without

---

*And if you know what that is, then I apologize for putting that visual in your brain.

medication and in near silence, but her attending nurses had been so impressed they'd dubbed her a "Hero Warrior Goddess."

I couldn't wait to be a Hero Warrior Goddess.

During the final class, after a little in-class potluck celebration that featured six varieties of lentil salad (and one box of Fig Newtons hastily thrown into a Tupperware bowl in an attempt to appear homemade—thanks, us!), Linneah showed us one more movie, the pièce of vidéo de résistance.

The documentary subject was a woman in labor awaiting the arrival of her midwife for what was to be a simple, sweet home birth with her husband and toddler by her side. But just as her contractions began to build, she learned that the midwife was having car trouble and would not likely make it in time.

I leaned forward on my yoga ball and watched through my fingers as the woman on the screen squatted on her bathroom floor. From behind the camera, a shaky male voice asked, "W-what do you want me to do?" The now-panting and mostly nude woman looked into the lens and answered, "Oh, just hold the camera." And then she proceeded to reach down and deliver the first baby.

Oh, did I fail to mention that she was giving birth to TWINS?

After handing off the first* baby to the father/cameraman, she then REACHED BACK UP INTO HERSELF and

---

*FIRST(!)

uttered a quiet but emphatic, "Ah, shit. She's breech" (i.e., upside down; i.e., not optimal; i.e., HOLY CRAP-CAKES).

This naked-from-the-waist-down Hero Warrior Goddess then delivered her second baby, single-handedly, deftly and ably, and, aside from a few well-placed grunts, without complaint. By the time the midwife (who really should be chewed out for not getting her oil checked before heading out to deliver a G.D. baby or two) showed up, there was nothing left for her to do, aside from enjoy a spot of tea along with a play-by-play of the missed event.

Aside from the fact that it was more dramatic than anything Michael Bay could pull out of his own vagina, watching that movie in Linneah's classroom that night instilled in me a powerful combination of confidence and self-assurance in my own ability to handle my impending labor. If this woman could self-deliver twins in her bathroom (and not a very big bathroom at that), surely I could deliver *one* baby in the comfort of a well-lit hospital with medical help, plenty of ice chips, a yoga ball, and *Austin Powers** playing in the background.

∿

---

*One of several comedy movies packed into our "birthing bag"; other movies included *Napoleon Dynamite, Anchorman,* and *Raising Arizona,* just in case it's true that, as Linneah said, "laughter is conducive to a painless labor." Other packed items included: one yoga ball upon which to bounce/relax/roll around to help ease contractions and to serve as a conversation starter with hospital staff ("Why, yes, I do yoga. I pretty much kill at Tree Pose"); one pair of flannel pajamas featuring an ironic cartoon skull pattern to indicate that even though I'm now a mom, I'm still hip and relevant; an iPod loaded with ten-plus hours of hypnobirthing audio tracks; and a selection of books and magazines to enjoy during all that "downtime" I was sure to have.

My due date came and went with not a contraction in sight, at which point a number of homeopathic "labor-inducing" tricks were employed. They included, but were not limited to:

- Some vigorous nonsexual massaging of my perineum (again, sorry), mostly by me, but occasionally by husband, on days that he could be persuaded with the aid of beer, ice cream, and/or the promise of sexual activity at some later date, TBD.
- The eating of a particular salad at a particular café in the San Fernando Valley said to guarantee labor within twenty-four hours. If "guaranteed labor" means uncontrollable gas for two days straight, then the salad was successful. Otherwise, it was not.
- "Uneven walking": the act of walking along a curb with one foot on the curb, the other on the street, in the style of a drunken sorority sister.
- "Cervical sweeps," an ob-gyn procedure/medieval torture by which one's doctor sweeps a gloved finger around the inside of one's bajingo, with the intention of "softening" or "ripening" the cervix, which, despite being a "natural," homeopathic technique, leaves one feeling as though one is a ventriloquist dummy and that someone is reaching up into one's soul by way of one's vagina.
- Sex. Lots and lots of it. Some good, some bad. Most of it very, very ugly.
- Yelling "COME ON ALREADY!!!" directly at my navel.

Unfortunately, none of these methods seemed to work, and after two more noncontraction-filled weeks passed, my doctor recommended induction with Pitocin.

"Marvelous," I said. "Let's get this party started so I can breathe this mo-fo out" (or words to that effect).

My doctor cautioned, "You should know that induction can be a little 'intense.'"

"Yeah?" I interrupted. "Well, so can I. LET'S DO THIS!!!"

The doctor interrupted my interruption, "You should also know that most induced women," 95 percent was the number he floated, "end up requesting an epidural* to control the pain." Sure, I thought. That's because 95 percent of women didn't spend five weeks listening to hypnosis tapes, learning how to breathe out their pain like wisps of multicolored smoke, or visualizing their babies rolling out of them like gentle waves of water.

I just smiled and said, "I'm not going to need the epidural. I'm pretty sure I'll be fine." And then I patted his arm in my most confident, bordering-on-condescending way.

⤳

Induction Day.

We are in the labor room. I am feeling confident, alert, alive. Like a quarterback ready to run, catch, and spike my team to victory. This is a great day to have a baby, and I mean that in the most crunchy-granola way possible.

---

*"Vagisthesia." You're welcome.

The doctor fills my IV with induction sauce, breaks my water, and informs me that the contractions should start any minute.

I stick my headphones in my ears, sit on my yoga ball, and begin to bounce while I wait for the first one, wondering whether it will feel like a wave or a surge, or maybe a strong splash? Luckily, I don't have to wait very long, because within thirty seconds the first contraction arrives, less like a surge or a wave and more like a canoe paddle being swung full force at the side of my head. My knees buckle, and I hit the deck with an all-over body sensation that is so intense the word *pain* does not do it justice; it requires a word that has not been invented yet, like *blundikad* or *krevdentious*. That's how beyond pain it is. It is *krevdentious*.

Sweat—not merely beads, but actual spigots of it— springs from every one of my pores, even as the contraction ebbs. From my mouth comes a yowl-y moan/scream, "EPIDUH-EPIDUH-EPIDUHHHHH," and my husband, whose face now looks like that of a scared rabbit says, "The epidural team is coming. Please let go of my arm."

But then, after I've had a few minutes to recover, in a startling turn of events that shocks even me, I tell my husband that no, I will *not* be needing the epidural. I just hadn't been *prepared* for that first one . . . Now that I *knew* what a contraction felt like, I was *sure* I could *handle* it.

I sit down on the yoga ball and brace myself for the next contraction that I am going to manage with the breathing and visualization exercises I've learned from Linneah.

In . . . Out . . . Gentle waves of water.

In . . . Out . . . Gentle waves of water.

In . . . Out . . . Gentle waves of water.

. . . And then the next canoe paddle wallops me upside the head and knocks me twenty thousand leagues under the sea, and that's when I reach for my husband with the strength of a rabid chimpanzee and instruct him to bring the epidural team to me within the next five minutes or I am going to tear the linoleum off the delivery-room floor and eat it.

Within minutes the team (there are two of them, and they work on me in tandem like a pair of circus acrobats) has me intubated, and they send the invisible canoe paddler on his way. From this point on, the delivery is a friggin party (the kind of party where people cheer when you poop on the table, anyway) and that's when the camera comes out.

+~+

Watching the video now, I feel so disconnected from those people on the screen. I don't remember any of it, even though consciously I know it happened, and there's plenty of proof—i.e., a small dictatorial human living in our house—to support that conclusion.

As I look at the image of my poor, poor crotch, so unaware of what is about to unfold . . . from its folds . . . I experience a level of discomfort probably not unlike what men must feel when witnessing other men being kicked in their baby-makers. I can't watch without wincing and squinting through one barely open eye, the way I might watch the outtakes of a *Jackass* movie or scenes from *The Texas Chainsaw Massacre*.

A blurry figure steps in front of the camera; I recognize it as my mother. My father, on the other hand, is not in attendance. This is probably for the best, as between the two of us, there has been no acknowledgment that I am, in fact, female.

My husband comments, "I forgot that part! Your mom stepped right in front of the camera—we almost missed the whole thing!" But to be honest, I am grateful to her backside for giving me even a brief reprieve from this Salvador-Dalí-melting-vulva horror show, the sight of which is now making me lightheaded.

⤳

"Okay, now I want you to push," says the doctor.

I am straining and pushing as hard as I can, so intensely that I feel something is bound to pop out of me, if not this kid, then possibly one of my eyeballs, or my spleen through my now-cartoonishly stretched-out belly button.

I can see the doctor, distorted through the edges of my oxygen mask, framed between the V of my shaking legs. He is talking to the husband, gesturing toward the surface underneath my butt. They are both nodding approvingly. It's difficult to make out exactly what the doctor is saying, though I can just hear the words *good sign, large amount,* and *rectum.*

⤳

Several hours of fecal/fetal pushing go by, and still the not-so-tiny human stuck in my undercarriage refuses to come out. Nothing changes.

Until it does.

⤳

Now some serious-type drama is going down.

1. The baby's heartbeat starts to drop. Quickly. Which causes:
2. The machines to beep insistently and:
3. The room to flood with doctors and nurses. In all the panic:
4. The grandma-to-be leaves the room. As she passes the camera, it is clear that she is crying.
5. And in the most clear indication that the shit is hitting the fan, the *Austin Powers* dvd is turned off.

The doctor says loudly and quite clearly that this baby has to come out now and that he is going to insert some sort of vacuum device inside my vagina to help ease her out. I say, "Okay," but when I see the size of the device, it seems as doable as trying to fit a frisbee into a jar of mustard.

More pushing and grunting and pushing and grunting, and then in an instant I feel the heat of a thousand suns in my nethers. And that's the moment that I become fully educated as to the precision of an epidural, i.e., it dulls sensation completely—but only up to a point. One millimeter beyond that, there is absolute, total, full-blown feeling. I have just gone, sensation-wise, from zero to *YAAAAARRRGHHHHH*!!!

(Much has been said about the noises that emanate/emerge/pour forth from a woman in labor. Having been raised on the Canadian prairies, I can say with authority that what I most sounded like in that moment was an angry moose about to crap a full-grown bear.)

And FLOP! out comes the kid, like a flying fish jumping into a rowboat. And in an instant, watching that video, I know exactly why we taped it. Because that moment is pure magic. She wasn't there . . . and then, she was. It didn't matter how it happened, whether naturally or with drugs or by hypnosis or silent chanting or with a set of pneumatic vacuum tubes like the ones they used to have at drive-thrus in the '70s. The only thing that matters is she's here.

That moment was—and still is, as pictured here on my computer screen—pure, breathtaking magic.

And then some more gross stuff comes out, and suddenly it's a party all over again. The grandma is laughing, the in-laws barge in, cameras start flashing . . .

In the video, the husband is rubbing my arm and kissing me. I am smiling and crying. He leans over and says over and over again, "She's perfect . . . She's perfect . . . "

Just watching it on my computer makes me tear up. I look at my husband sitting next to me, glassy-eyed and beaming at the video screen. I smile at him and say the only thing that makes sense:

"YOU SAPPY BASTARD!!"

᚛ *three* ᚜

SPOILED MILK

My breasts* have always been my best quality. I'm not bragging when I say that; they're just great relative to the rest of my body, which is a gallery of horrors in comparison. There are so many problems with what's below my belly button there's not time enough to list it all (although if you're familiar with the myth of Medusa, then you've got a pretty good idea of what it looks like inside my underwear). By default, my breasts were my best girls, and historically the first things to be

---

*Boobs, tits, ta-ta's, "the girls," chesticles, naughty pillows, "Buddy & Bernice." These are all phrases I wanted to use in this story but which my editor advised against, on the basis that their usage would make me seem immature. To which I responded, "You're worried *that's* what's going to make me seem immature? Do you even know me?!"

revealed on a blind date, a game of strip poker, or during a sale at The Home Depot.

There was no reason to believe that my breasts wouldn't be up to the task of nourishing the new human that I (with a little help from the husband) had created. And oh, they were! Because after the epidural worked its rubber-legged magic, and after I took a breath and squeezed out that nine-pound, ten-ounce baby like I'd squeeze a watermelon seed through my fingers, the kid latched onto my nipple and nursed like she'd been doing it all her life (which, if you do the math, she had).

I'm not sure if there does exist an actual "Mother of the Year" award-giving body, but if there is, I was well on my way to winning, if not a Lifetime Achievement Award, then at least a sweet Runner-Up Plaque.

That is, until our one-week pediatrician appointment revealed that our perfect baby had lost 20 percent of her birth weight—double what was acceptable. "Failure to thrive," he called it. Even though she was nursing every three hours, she was literally starving.

My breasts were a bust.*

The pediatrician suggested we switch to formula right way.

Whoa, Dr. Cowboy! This is not my beautiful motherhood experience. I know what happens to children who don't breast-feed. They become drug addicts, serial killers, and socialites. I know that Michael Jordan was breast-

---

*That might be the best/worst pun I've ever made. My sincere apologies.

fed until he was three and that Charles Manson was not breast-fed at all. But since I was two hundred years too late to locate a wet nurse, I conceded to give the child formula, but only until she had gained the requisite amount of weight. After that I was determined to breast-feed my baby for one year, minimum.

It was suggested that I visit a lactation consultant by the name of Binky. If Binky wasn't available, I was to see Corky. Those names are so real I don't even have a joke worthy of them.

We drove to Binky's office in the San Fernando Valley, whereupon she proceeded to examine my breast-feeding technique. Her findings? What was coming out of my nipples was something closer to puffs of milk-scented air than actual milk. My supply "sucked." That was the bad news. The good news is that it was the baby's fault, not mine.

The baby had a bad latch, which led to my breasts being engorged, which led to my milk supply drying up, which led to my sitting in a small windowless office while a grown woman named Binky milked me.

That's right. I was milked by a Binky.

Binky grabbed my nipple and pinched it hard—I realize this sounds like porn for Teletubbies, but it was about as sexy as back acne, (i.e., not at all*).

She grabbed my nipple and jammed it about twelve inches into the baby's mouth. At that moment, the moment

---

*Unless you're into that sort of thing. And if you are, then (a) each to his own and (b) Blortch.

of my first proper latch, it became clear to me that my baby was part piranha. I'm not sure how I managed to conceive a child with the genes of a carnivorous freshwater fish from South America, but it seemed the only way to explain the excruciating pain.

I stamped my foot on the floor repeatedly, mostly to keep myself from punching my baby in the face. (Truth is, I would never punch my baby. I may, however, wait until she's fifteen years old and give her one retroactively. I'm fairly certain she'll deserve it by then anyway.)

Two hours and several hundred dollars later, Binky sent us away with a hospital-grade pump, which I was to use every three hours until my supply could match my daughter's demand.

When we got home, the husband bottle-fed the baby while I zipped on my hands-free pumping bra, turned on the pump, and then watched it stretch my nipples through a transparent sleeve, like Augustus Gloop going through the pipes of Willy Wonka's chocolate river.

Now that I could actually see the milking process, I understood the problem. Milk wasn't flowing, it was eking out of my nipples, like tiny beads of Elmer's glue. One hour of Hoover-strength milking left me with a grand total of a half-ounce of milk. And most of that came from the right breast; the left was completely useless. If my right breast was a slacker, my left was its illiterate cousin who lost half his brain in a tragic pig-farming accident.

But I would not be beaten. Over the next few weeks the husband bottle-fed the child, while I pumped every three to four hours for up to an hour at a time.

I learned all about "galactagogues," which, though it sounds like an alien form of governance, is actually any substance that encourages lactation. As a result, I ate oatmeal in large amounts, drank Guinness beer in small amounts, and ingested an herb that made my skin smell like a combination of maple syrup and curry (mostly curry).

I took a prescription medication for reflux, one side effect of which is increased lactation, another side effect of which is depression. A positively hilarious situation for a new mother, if you think about it!

I went to breast-feeding support groups and listened to other new moms complain about their problems with excessive flow, saying things like "Ah-ma-gad! I am literally gussshhhing! I'm storing the excess in our freezer—looks like we'll be drinking breast milk with our coffee for the next twenty years!" I smiled with empathy while imagining punching them in their overflowing gazongas.*

But mostly I pumped. And pumped. And pumped. And pumped.

Until little by little, drop by drop, my milk started to flow—or at least dribble. Not nearly at the rate the child was drinking, but enough that I could supplement her formula feedings with a little of my own milky love.

---

*Gazongas. I'd forgotten that one.

I was winning. Soon we would be the very picture of skin-to-skin maternal bliss.

But, as one slow-flowing nipple said to the other, "not so fast."

The child did not want the breast.

When I offered my ever-so-feebly lactating nipple to my daughter, she would give it a look and a suck and then scream into it like a rapper yelling into a microphone. Sometimes I'd try to fool her by making her laugh, and while her mouth was open I'd jam my nipple in there. But she never took to it. Instead, she'd just stare at me like I was some kind of sick pervert.

The worst part was that she could be calmed only by the *other* Binky, her pacifier: i.e., a silicone version of my nipple. This is what is known in the breast-feeding world as "nipple confusion." But if you'd asked my daughter, she would've said there was no confusion. That savvy four-week-old knew exactly what she wanted, and she couldn't have been clearer if she'd e-mailed her thoughts to me and b.c.c.'ed her lawyer. It was hard not to take it personally—almost as hard as it is to saw through a silicone pacifier with a steak knife.

I continued to pump around the clock and would then pour my liquid gold into little bottles that the husband would then feed her. I did this for five months until it occurred to me that the six hours a day I was spending with the pump might be better spent with my child. As much as I believe in the benefits of breast-feeding, I believe in the benefits of bonding even more.

That's when I eighty-sixed the pump, and from five months of age, my kid became 100 percent formula fed. That was five years ago, and now she's a happy, healthy, lovely child, and I'm at peace with my choice to abandon breast-feeding.*

---

*And that last part is a complete lie.

Back when she was still on the "F" (formula) I had a recurring nightmare about a citywide chemical explosion after which robots would take over the water supply and my baby would die because I wouldn't be able to feed her during the ensuing apocalypse.

Now I have more rational concerns . . . like the fact that having been robbed of her mother's milk she'll become a high school dropout and date a guy with a tattoo of a snake on his face who will try to rob a liquor store and accidentally shoot and kill kindly old Sheriff Jenkins and my dumdum of a daughter will get blamed for it and end up on death row where Susan Sarandon will try but ultimately fail to spare her life, leaving me to attempt a poorly planned prison break that will end with my death in a fiery hail of gunfire.

Of course I recognize this anxiety for what it is—an absurd and totally irrational fear that has no basis in reality but is predicated on an insidious set of cultural beliefs, which contribute to the notion that there exists a "perfect" style of mothering, but which of course we can all see is "perfect" only in that it is "perfectly" unattainable.

On the other hand—if I do die trying to bust my daughter out of prison, I think I can safely say that that "Mother of the Year" Award is mine.

four

SEXUAL DISINTERCOURSE

SOMETIME IN 1982
3:17 A.M.

I am awakened from a dream that involves me and one of the Hardy Boys engaged in a spicy bout of tonsil hockey. I sit up and stumble groggily out of bed and into the bathroom.

Sit. Pee. Wipe.

Stand. Wobble. Flush.

Still half-asleep, I put my hand on the bathroom door-knob to return to bed (and to a shirtless Sean Cassidy, I hope) when I hear coming from my parents' room what sounds like furniture being dropped on the floor. Repeatedly, rhythmically, and with great effort.

Fully awake now, I jerk my hand from the doorknob, as though a chemical fire is raging on the other side. I drop to the floor and pull the nubby, mildewy bath mat over my head. And there I wait until I am certain that the banging has stopped. And then I wait thirty minutes more, until I am absolutely, positively sure that I am the only one still awake in this house, and that no one will ever know, that I now know, what my parents were doing under their polyester comforter that night.*

↜↝

If I'd have been younger, the fact that my parents engaged in sexual congress probably wouldn't have phased me, and I would have skipped happily back to my room not caring that my father and mother were knocking boots just six feet away, on the other side of my pink cloud–mural-covered wall.

But at fifteen years old, the majority of my waking activities were centered on the topic of sex. Thinking about it. Dreaming about it. Looking it up in the school library dictionary, multiple times a day. Writing it in my notebooks so that I could study those three illicit letters arranged in such a filthy order.

So this sudden awareness that my parents were freely enjoying it—with each other, no less—it was a living, (heavy) breathing, gag-inducing nightmare. Because as anyone with a pituitary gland knows, there is nothing

---

*Until today, anyway.

more disturbing to a teenager than the knowledge that your parents have sex.*

But the lasting impact of this decades-old memory goes beyond my horrified fifteen-year-old self. Yes, the memory of it still gives me the sensation of having eaten raw chicken, but more than that I am left with an overwhelming feeling of wonderment and the enduring question: how did they do it?†

How did they—having been married, at the time, for more than twenty years—find the interest, the energy, and the will to do it?

SOME VERY UNSCIENTIFIC RESEARCH FROM A NOT-SO-RELIABLE SOURCE WITH FAIRLY LOOSE TIES TO REALITY

Leaving the example of my parents for a moment (and which I must if I am ever to properly digest a meal again), let's ponder the usual course of monogamous sex:

In the beginning phases, a typical monogamous sexual relationship is rife with newness, discovery, and laser-powered lust. There's a fire in each of your respective loins, and when you rub them together it's like starting a barbecue with truck-stop fireworks and diesel fuel. Your face is chapped raw from cheek to chin, you're bragging to friends about your weekly bladder infections, and the sound of your beloved's voice is like that of an angel singing . . . in the nude . . . with a boner.

---

*Okay, the sudden, irrefutable awareness that one day you and everyone you know will die—maybe that's worse (see Chapter 24). But undeniable proof that your parents are Going Down to Funkytown? That's an easy second.

†Not specifically, I should say (please God, no), as the merest hint of graphic detail would send me into a spontaneous coma.

Compare this to what happens after you've taken on the shared responsibility of parenthood:

You forget the basics of human grooming, allowing the hair on your body to grow so long that from behind you could be/have been mistaken for an elderly Greek man. You choose a self-initiated tax audit over being intimate with your spouse. And the sound of your beloved's voice is as pleasing as a dental instrument being jammed into your ear canal . . . in the nude . . . with a boner.

All of which begs the question: What the crap is going on here?!

Well, according to science,* married couples with children report significantly lower rates of sexual satisfaction than married couples without children.

In other words:

often leads to
SEXY SEX ⟶ BABY

totally annihilates
BABY ⟶ SEXY SEX

And Boom, there it is.

According to science, children steal your sex life, those adorably selfish little buggers. They impede the very act that created them, with unspoken and ironic delight.

But why? Why does passion fade like a jean jacket from H&M after just three days of wear? How is it possible that one minute you're unable to keep your hands off each

*Although I am not a professional scientist, I did major in theater with a minor in chemistry, so I'm practically a Rhodes scholar.

other, and the next you've forgotten that you possess com-
patible naked parts under your clothes?*

"WHY, OH WHY, DOES THE BOINKING GO BUH-BYE?"

In order to answer this question, let's break it down with
a few more very unscientific observations:

YOUR SHRINKING BANDWIDTH

This new human interloper is commanding a large chunk
of your time—time that you once used for a variety of important activities, like personal hygiene, keeping up with
those pesky Kardashians, and taking naked running leaps
onto your boyfriend. Now all of these activities are fighting for the limited time you have between diaper changes,
staring at your angry nipples, being cornered by dead-
eyed Stepford moms at the playground, and remembering
how letters combine to form words.†

"REAL" YOU, MEET YOUR "REAL" PARTNER

Before the kid showed up, parental stress was purely the-
oretical. Once that kid arrived, the poopoo hit the fan, lit-

---

*Note: There will be those among you (like you there, laying on your
purple-velvet chaise lounge, wearing slinky lingerie, fluffy high-heeled
slippers, and spritzing yourself with bottles of Eau d'Ohhh-Face) saying,
"That's not us. Our love life hasn't changed one bit. In fact, I'm stretching
out my sex muscles right now in anticipation of the marathon boink fest
we're going to enjoy later this afternoon." Listen, I applaud you. Really, I
do. But you are as normal and average as a sparkly, talking, rainbow-maned
unicorn. Please, do us all a favor and go, make dreams come true for your
lottery-winning partner. The rest of us will be here, working through our
based-in-reality problems.

†If you can read this, please disregard that last example. And also: thank
a teacher.

erally, figuratively, and with shocking frequency. You now find yourself facing new challenges every day, many of which you will not handle well (i.e., "Is that a diaper rash? Call 911!"). As a result, your co-parent may be left wondering why s/he ever found you sexable in the first place. (In my case, I'd guess that my husband was not exactly filled with desire for me the day that he watched me cuss out, kick, and cry at a stroller that wouldn't fold properly.)

SUBCONSCIOUS RESENTMENT

Far be it from me to put words in your mouth, but could it be that, in helping to bring this new game-changing person into your family, you subconsciously blame your mate for ruining your life? And while I'm gently depositing phrases into your oral cavity, may I also suggest that maybe you don't feel like having sex right now because (a) you don't want to risk this kind of thing happening again and (b) you'll be damned if you're going to give that bitch/bastard/jerk/effing effer even one effing iota of pleasure anytime this effing century.

NATURE IS FINISHED WITH YOU

As I've said before, what I know about science could probably half fill a small notebook, but that doesn't stop me from making grand generalizations about things that other people spend lifetimes studying. Hence my conclusion that once you've satisfied your hormonal imperative and are in the process of raising a child, "nature" has a waning interest in your continuing to reproduce and therefore hits the kill switch on the old libido machine and sends you off to find a new purpose. Like blogging about needlepoint. Or mastering chair yoga.

CONFLICTING EMOTIONS

Many couples experience difficulty adjusting to their dramatically changed roles. You may have trouble enjoying the image of your baby's father engaged in something that, only months ago, would have driven you wild with desire (i.e., that time he wore a rhinestone-studded G-string and gave you a lap dance to Def Leppard's "Pour Some Sugar on Me"). Similarly, your partner may now have trouble accepting the image of you as a sweet, loving mother figure when just last year he celebrated you in the heat of passion by yelling, "HOLY SCHNIKES, YOU COULD SUCK THE GLAZE OFF MY GRANDMA'S HUMMEL FIGURINES!"

OLD COPING MECHANISMS NO LONGER APPLY

Back in the prekid days, when you and your partner quarreled over something important,* you could make a dramatic exit, then return twelve hours later with a new outlook and some cheap wine in your gullet, raring to go for some exhausting and satisfying makeup sex. But all that's off the table now. What made for "hot drama" before—slamming doors, dramatic ultimatums, disappearing into the night—has morphed into "irresponsible parenting" at best and "child endangerment" at worst. Not cool, man. *Not cool.*

---

*Like, for example, how to correctly load a dishwasher; or whether KISS is the greatest rock act in history. Or not.

Your Home Has Been Overtaken by the Detritus of Babyhood

No more lava-lamp lighting or sensual Patrick Nagel prints on the wall; your love den has been transformed into a waypoint for thousands of dollars of unsexy, plastic-molded, primary-colored crap. That leopard-print love seat on which you once posed seductively? It's now home to a pile of stained baby bibs. That groovy beanbag chair in which the two of you used to get nasty? It's now covered in a layer of mysterious and foul-smelling slime. And if you do somehow manage to get your cranky, tired engines started, you can look forward to rolling over onto a radio-controlled triceratops and pinching a spinal nerve in the aftermath. And trust me—I speak from experience when I say that it's near impossible to keep your motor running after pulling a piece of Lego out of your butt crack.

As the previous examples clearly illustrate, parental lovemaking is like a rare, endangered ferret that must be caught, cornered, and beaten into submission if one is ever to enjoy its fruits again.

But beat it we must. Because in any long-term relationship, sex is like the glue that holds together that unsightly Ikea bookcase you've had since college. Sure, it's cheap, ugly, and it doesn't match the decor—but it's keeping everything in order. And yes, you could buy something newer and more expensive, but why bother? We're all gonna be dead soon anyway.

That is why I have devised a helpful list of activities, many of which I have personally attempted, to help you reintroduce the ever-elusive parental grinding back into your life.

IDEAS FOR REANIMATING THE CORPSE THAT WAS ONCE YOUR SEX LIFE

TAKE A CLASS TOGETHER

Nothing stokes the home fires like learning a new skill side by side. The husband and I recently started taking classes in the martial art of Tae Kwon Do. It's gratifying to grow with him, to share in the struggle of this unfamiliar skill, and celebrate together as we develop and evolve in our abilities. It's also gratifying to surprise him when he comes out of the shower with a roundhouse kick to his solar plexus.

Check your local community college for other potentially sexy shared educational opportunities—some ideas: Accounting 101, Spot Welding, Small Animal Veterinary Surgery, and the Art and Science of Hostage Negotiation.

BE A LOVER AND A FIGHTER

It's a well-known fact that Makeup Sex is the third-best sex there is[*]—so don't wait for a fight to happen organically; go out and pick one. Here are some helpful starter lines that have worked for me:

- "Last night I had a dream that you cheated on me. YOU BASTARD!"

---

[*]Behind (1) furtive sex with a member of your wedding party and (2) groupie sex with Mick Jagger, circa 1970. (Note: I have no personal experience with either of the foregoing.)

- "The toilet paper goes over, not under. What are you, some kind of maniac?"
- "Wow. I never noticed how far apart your eyes are."

You might also try making rude comments about your mother-in-law, unless your spouse doesn't get along with his or her mother, in which case you could speak at length about your mother-in-law's wonderful qualities or simply wear one of her cardigans to bed.

THE ELEMENT OF SURPRISE

No one wants to knock boots with predictable, sensible footwear. So keep your partner guessing, not just at night-time but throughout the day:

- wake your spouse in the morning with a kiss and a loving blast from an air horn
- give him/her a sultry look while stirring relish into his/her morning coffee
- cover his/her eyes and play "Guess Who!" at un-predictable times, like when he/she's attempting to merge on the freeway, or just as he/she's about to go under for a colonoscopy exam

BABY YOUR SPOUSE

Many partners feel neglected with the arrival of a needy new family member in the house. Make sure your spouse knows that you love him just as much as the new baby by cooking a romantic dinner and spoon-feeding it to him (steak, wine, and chocolate makes for a very sexy combo, especially when puréed into a blended smoothie). Other options: diaper your spouse, wear him around the house in a Baby Bjorn (size XXXL), or Ferberize him.

ROLE-PLAY AND FANTASY

Fantasy is a wonderful tool for injecting a little fun into your relationship—feel free to incorporate elements from real life:

* Role-play that she's the admissions officer for the preschool you're really hoping to get into. Slip an extra hundred into your partner's palm as you shake hands and leave the meeting.
* Pretend you're the babysitter—because when you get down to it, male or female, straight or gay, who doesn't fantasize about making love to an eastern European grandma type who smells of mothballs and stewed chicken liver?

THE WAY TO HIS HEART IS THROUGH HIS STOMACH VIA HIS GROIN

Enjoy Breakfast-and-a-Whole-Lot-More-in-Bed before the children awaken. Take into account that you'll need time to prepare breakfast (45 mins), eat it (2.5 mins), actual hanky-panky time (20 secs–160 mins: your mileage may vary), postpanky shower and cleanup (75 mins). For best results, set alarm clock for 2:45 A.M.

✦〜✦

Although it's very easy for parents to watch their sexual lives turn into a vast wasteland of complacency, boredom, and, in extreme cases, hymen regrowth, I hope I've convinced you that it doesn't have to be that way. All it takes is the motivation, a little imagination, and some judicious time management (as well as a collection of wigs, a high-speed blender, and a medium-size investment at your local mom-and-pop sex shop).

five

HUSSSSH

I'm lying on the floor, impressions of a shag rug embedded in my cheek. I'm not sure how long I've been here, but judging from the six-inch-wide wet spot under my chin, it seems I must have passed out some time ago.

But even though my shoulder is jacked and my bladder's about to burst, I'm staying right where I am. I've come too far to change course now.

~+

Parenthood in the twenty-first century is a never-ending obstacle course through a brier patch of thorny topics. Cloth diapers versus Disposable. Circumcision versus Natural. Breast-feeding versus Formula. Piercing your baby's ears versus Piercing your baby's navel.

"Sleep Training"—also known as the "Cry It Out" method—is the latest hot-button issue. Some consider it a sin of great magnitude, somewhere between formula feeding and leaving your kid in the backyard tied up to a tree.

The general gist behind "crying it out" is[*]

1. After five months of age, it's generally safe for babies to go eight hours without eating. In order to do that, all you have to do is:
    A. wean them off nighttime feedings; when they wake up in the middle of the night and begin to cry, you simply
        a. ignore them, and eventually,
            i. they'll get the idea that crying is getting them nowhere, at which point they'll throw up their tiny hands, say "Ah, screw it," and then they'll roll over and start sleeping through the night.

As much as I pride myself on being a badass who can handle anything,[†] even this sounds especially brutal to me.

But for us, lack of sleep has become the thorniest thorn in our well-pricked sides. The kid, now six months old, is

---

[*]Although I fancy myself a genius of the MacArthur magnitude, I am not a trained medical professional; please take everything you read here with a Donald Trump–head-size grain of salt, and talk to your own doctor, do your own research. I am not—I repeat, NOT—to be trusted. Thank you. Now carry on.

[†]Anything, that is, except for the sound of my parents enjoying sexual relations.

incapable of sleeping more than three hours at a time. As a result, the husband and I bicker constantly over whose turn it is to get her, based on such arguments as "I got her last time," "I have to work in the morning," and "But I'm the one with a family history of brain aneurysms," and I am now losing what remains of my already stretched paper-thin mind.

A few weeks ago I found myself in the living room, awake at two in the morning, with the baby sound asleep in my arms. I sat on the couch and began watching *Reservoir Dogs,* one of Quentin Tarantino's more delicate films, as a treat to myself after a long day of momming. An hour or so into the movie, I happened to glance down at the kid and saw that her eyes were wide open and trained on the spectacle of Michael Madsen hacking off some poor bastard's ear. This threw me into a panic because, as everybody knows, being exposed to violence at so young an age may/can/most certainly will turn a baby into a sociopath.

"Now I've done it," I thought. "I've broken the kid." And then I landed on an ingenious idea: Maybe if I press on the soft spot of her head, that will erase the memory . . . because didn't I once read somewhere that it's like a human "delete" key?

Now, the important thing to know is that I did NOT press on my baby's soft spot in order to purge a violent movie scene from her memory. But I did think about it. For a solid three minutes. Which is why I spent the entire morning of the following day researching the topic of "Sleep Training."

～

A friend turns me on to a dog-eared spiral-bound hand-book that espouses a "gentler" sleep-training technique— the idea being that you put the kid in its crib at bedtime, stand in the doorway, and offer some verbal assurance that "Mommy will be right outside," that kind of thing, but—and this is important—no touching. You close the door, and if (when) the kid starts to cry, you do exactly *nothing* for precisely five minutes, at which point you poke your head into the room—again, without touch-ing the kid—and say, "I'm here, all is well, everything's gonna be okay, buh-bye now," and after thirty reassuring seconds at most (NO TOUCHING!), you close the door. This time you let the kid cry for ten minutes before going in again and giving brief, loving, verbal reassurances.

Lather, rinse, add five more minutes, repeat.

There's a little more to the setup (some stuff about sleep routines and "dream feedings"),* but those are the broad strokes. The theory is that for the overwhelming majority of babies, it should take three days until they're able to fall asleep without crying and make it through the night without waking; some die-hards may take up to five days. One child was said to have taken a week, though clearly this was some überintense, sub- (or maybe super-) human kid.

This is where the differences in our (my husband's and my) parenting styles come into play, for if it were up

---

*Dream feeding: the act of bottle or breast-feeding an infant while it's still asleep, much like that time in college you awoke to realize that you'd eaten four Nutrisystem bars and a mostly melted half gallon of Chunky Monkey ice cream in your sleep.

to the husband, we'd continue to wake up every three hours to feed and cuddle the kid, up to her freshman year in college.

Luckily, it's not up to him—and so we embark on "Operation For-the-Love-of-God-Go-to-Sleep."

On the first night, forty-five seconds after she begins to cry, the husband pushes past me, picks up the child, and hugs her to his chest, glaring at me as if I'm some sort of crazed dolphin killer. He tells me I must have read the book wrong and implies that I have done permanent damage to the child.

Several days of sleeplessness later, he breaks down and is ready to try again. This time he makes it to the three-minute mark before aggressively shoving me out of the way and rescuing the crying baby.

A week later, with a level of exhaustion that I've never known (something akin to what I'm guessing the Sherpas of Everest must experience), we give it one more go. This time I banish the husband to our bedroom with a pair of noise-canceling headphones and a DVD of *The Matrix* (parts 1, 2, and 3) and tell him, "No matter what you hear beyond these walls, do not open this door." Torn between his principles and a not-so-secret obsession with Carrie-Ann Moss, he reluctantly agrees and shuts the door behind him. I consider padlocking him inside but decide that's probably a little extreme. Also, we don't have any padlocks.

I lay the baby down in her crib, close the door, and then set the timer on my phone for five minutes. Right on cue, she begins to cry.

You just don't realize the absolute power of your baby's cry until you willfully ignore it. Nature knew what it was doing when it picked that particular combination of sounds (pathetic, indignant, and loud) that tug at something deep within me, somewhere between my cervix and my spleen.

It's hard to take, especially knowing that the immediate remedy for the sound coming out of her would be for me to just go in there and pick her up. But our long-term sanity, her health and welfare, and the integrity of her soft little delete key—not to mention the intensity of my need to be right all the time—all of it depends on this plan working.

I make a pact with myself that, whatever happens, I will be strong. And instead of merely blocking out the sound of her cries, I take a Zen approach and listen intently, really hearing her. It is then that I become aware of how impressively varied and expressive her cries are.

What follows is an approximate translation of those first five minutes:

"Wah? . . ."	*Why hast thou forsaken me?*
"WAH!!!"	*WHERE THE FRIG ARE YOU?!*
"Muhhhh?"	*I can hear you skulking around out there—guess you should have opted for carpet over bare wood floors. Now stop screwing around and get in here NOW.*
	I need to be jiggled.
"Eeeeeh-UHHH!"	*Please? I love you. No, I don't. I hate your guts.*

"Wahhhhaaaa . . . "	*I'm sorry . . . I didn't mean when I said I hated your guts. I understand this is difficult for you, but if you'd just open that door, I'm sure we could work this out together.*
"WAHHHHH!!!!"	*I WILL KILL YOU IN YOUR SLEEP!!!*

Finally, the five-minute timer goes off with an *AWOOOOOGAH*! (because yes, I am the person who uses the old-timey car horn as my ring tone).

I open the door and stick my head into her room. She stops midcry, standing in her crib, red-faced and startled, as though I've just caught her shoplifting. I say the thing that I'm supposed to say, to the effect of "Hi sweetie, Mommy's here, everything's okay. Nighty-night." And then I step out and close the door behind me.

Now she is *pissed*. She has very clearly picked up on the fact that she is being manipulated, and she is so very NOT down with it. She continues screaming, though now she has added a new sound into the mix, an indignant, growly screech that would be perfect if she were the lead singer of an '80s death-metal band. Which, to my knowledge, she is not.

The next ten minutes are endless and pass with all the ease of a Pap-smear exam. I pace around the hallway, listening to her shrieks and trying hard to remember if *The Exorcist* was based on factual source material.

At the ten-minute mark—*AWOOOOOGAH*!—I open the door to her room. Her face is moist with tears and sweat; she's angry and exhausted. I know that face; I've seen it in the mirror a thousand times, on the heels of a thousand rage-filled disappointments.

I step into the room and say some more soothing words; I set the timer on my phone, and again I close the door. I consider yanking the husband out of his Carrie-Anne Moss–filled cocoon so that I can get some moral support— but no. I will do this alone. And once it's over, I will gloat about having done so.

And then something miraculous happens. Within a few minutes her cries taper off and transition to deep, snore-y breaths. She is actually falling asleep.

But just as her breaths grow slower and longer, an insistent new sound erupts, this one from the house next door. I sprint on tiptoes to the bathroom and peek through the blinds, through which I can see the neighbor, not five feet away, inside her house, busily vacuuming the wall.

I can't quite process what I'm seeing. It's eight o'clock at night. And the sound is so loud, it seems she's vacuuming marbles out of her drapes. WHY ARE THERE MARBLES IN HER DRAPES?! I knock on the window, but of course she can't hear through the G.D. marbles . . .

If a baby's cry is the most powerful sound in all of humanity, then the second most powerful sound is me whisper-yelling through two panes of glass, "IF YOU DON'T TURN OFF THAT VACUUM CLEANER, THEN I AM COMING TO YOUR HOUSE WITH AN ARMLOAD OF DIRTY DIAPERS AND I'M LEAVING EMPTY-HANDED!!"*

---

*I may not have yelled the part about the diapers, but I thought it very loudly.

Perhaps she heard me—or perhaps she didn't hear me and it was just the specter of my psychotic, snarling face through the blinds, looking like some sort of deranged toilet demon . . . Whatever it was, it worked. The vacuum cleaner gets switched off.

I listen at the child's door; miraculously (and luckily for our marble-sucking neighbor), it appears she is still sleeping.

I turn to check the timer on my phone—then realize I don't have my phone.

My phone.

I have left my phone in the baby's room. With the timer running. The timer that will count down to zero and then end with the blaring horn of a 1923 Packard.

I have to get it out of there in the next . . . I'm not sure—I started it at fifteen minutes, maybe we're at six minutes now? . . . without waking her. This will be tricky.

With incredible precision (of an order that would put Carrie-Ann Moss to shame), I enter the child's room using the slow, silent, walking-against-the-wind skills I honed back when I was a professional mime.* I can hear the gentle *shhnooooccchh* of her sleepy breaths. I can see, too, the light of my phone on the changing table where I'd set it down without thinking.

As I grab the phone and switch off the timer, the child stirs and turns over. I dive onto the shaggy throw rug where I refrain from moving until I am certain she is still asleep.

---

*This is not a lie; I actually was a professional mime.

Lying on the floor, I am surprised at how comfortable I am; that mime bit really took it out of me—it may have been the most actual exercise I've done all year. The child's overpriced tea-towel-size crib blanket has fallen onto the floor, so I pull it over me (over one-quarter of my torso, anyway), and I begin to drift off to sleep—which doesn't seem like the worst idea I've had today, so . . .

What the hell. I let it happen.

~

I am awakened. By my bladder. I have to pee, urgently and with the intensity of a blocked fire hose. I can tolerate sleeping on my face next to an overflowing diaper pail on carpet that hasn't been vacuumed in two years, but I draw the line at lying in my own urine. I would try peeing into (onto? at?) one of the baby's ultra-absorbent diapers, but the fresh ones are out of arm's reach.

I have to get out of here. But the hallway light that would have lit my escape route is no longer on. The husband must have turned it off, the thoughtful bastard, and now I find myself in a pitch-black abyss.

I begin to feel my way across the toy-strewn floor, crawling on my belly toward the door, when my knee hits something. I cast my eye downward and see a small multi-colored ray of light begin to flash. And then . . .

"TWIN-KLE TWIN-KLE! LITTLE STA-AAR! HOW I WON-DER WHA-AAA—"

It's that goddamn singing drum! I throw myself on top of it, hoping that my muffin-top flab will stifle the sound while I search frantically for the off switch. Why must every toy sing? And always in the same voice, some wannabe country star who sings every song with far too much sincerity and earnestness and ohmygod I'm gonna fly to Nashville and find her so I can rip out her vocal chords and make sure she never sings another G.D. note!

The toy stops its squeal-singing . . . and then switches abruptly to singing in Spanish (still the same woman, Ay Dios Mio)! I claw at the toy, locate the power switch again, this time turning it OFF.

The crib springs creak as the kid's 20-pound frame bolts upright.

I can see the whites of her enormous eyes glinting in the darkness.

"Mmmuh? Mmmuh?"

I slide the tiny blanket over my face and hold my breath.

She's looking in my direction—but I don't think she's actually seeing me. Maybe she's not quite awake yet, or perhaps her eyes have not adjusted to the dark, or maybe it's that she's six months old and for all she knows it's totally normal for floors to suddenly grow 125-pound lumps in them.* †

I'm not sure what to do if she starts to cry. The pamphlet didn't say anything about how to handle being caught in the act; if I reveal myself to her, will she be confused or alarmed? Or will she simply come to believe that her parents are always with her, hiding under her bed?‡

---

*All right, 129-pound lumps.
†Fine. 137.
‡Maybe not such a bad thing in about ten years.

I stay where I am, frozen in space and time, my full-to-bursting bladder pressing against my corneas. All I can do is lay here with my thoughts, most of which involve rushing water.

The child begins to babble to herself. Normally, I love the sound of her nonsense talking—when she does it, I like to imagine that she's addressing Congress—but now I'm terrified that her thoughts on the Health Care Bill will transform into wails.

Thankfully, this doesn't happen. Instead, she lies down, her babbling softening until it is just soft, whispery breaths. After I am certain that she is asleep, I get up off the floor and sneak out. And just as I am about to shut her bedroom door, I find myself face-to-face with the husband, who is now en route to the toilet.

"IS SHE OUT?" he croaks loudly.

If I could think of a way to throttle the life out of him in total silence, I would. Unfortunately, I am not a martial arts expert,* so instead I push past him to the bathroom, where I release my bodily fluids, as slowly and quietly as I can.

～

The next morning when I walk into the child's room, she coos and beams at me with those big, bright eyes, the ones that just ten hours ago appeared to be plotting my demise. I am amazed that she doesn't seem to be holding a grudge about last night—though that may simply be

---

*Yet.

because she hasn't yet developed the language skills to tell me to go to hell.

Incredibly, the dog-eared book with questionable origins is right; by the third night, she goes down without crying and sleeps all the way through until morning. Just days later her father and I are well-rested and getting along much better, and when we do bicker, we cover a much wider and more interesting array of topics. Still, I'd like to believe that this experience won't leave any permanent traces on her memory. I sincerely hope so, because now I've got no other means to counteract them; her soft spot has long since disappeared.

✢ six ✢

HOW NOT TO CALM
A CHILD ON A PLANE

I am at the airport with my daughter and the guy she calls "Dada." We are about to board a Florida-bound plane to visit my mother-in-law.

But the toddler is losing her shit.

After two years of being the perfect travel companion, she has suddenly developed a fear of flying. I wonder if maybe she's worked out the physics of what we are about to do. Perhaps she has come to realize, as I have, that manned flight is a practical impossibility and is certain to end in our fiery deaths. Or maybe she's just toying with me. Whatever is going on in that reptilian brain of hers, she is yelling at the top of her lungs, "NO AY-PWAY! NO

53

AY-PWAYYYYY!" as we board the aircraft and take refuge in our seats.

Luckily, we've scored the bulkhead. Actually, luck had nothing to do with it. I had flirted mercilessly with the ticketing agent, a very fit man with impeccable hair, who my husband later informed me was clearly gay. But whether I'd seduced him, or whether he'd simply taken pity on a woman with zero gaydar, the result was the same: I'd scored. But in this moment I take no comfort in our rock-star seating, because there is a demon in my lap who is trying to separate my scalp from my head.

People file past us, with varying looks of pity and horror but mostly relief that they're not sitting next to the kid who's screaming like a mongoose that's been stabbed with a rusty steak knife. And even though the titanium-haired stewardess has announced that the flight is full, the seat next to me remains suspiciously empty. Perhaps my neighbor-to-be saw the Tasmanian Devil in my arms, then chose to deplane and take the ninety-six-hour Greyhound bus ride home instead.

At this point the husband and I do the only thing we *can* do: we turn on each other. He glares at me and I glare back, an exchange that every parent recognizes as the "I WILL DIVORCE YOU IN THE NEXT FOUR SECONDS UNLESS YOU FIX THIS" glare.

His response is to rub her back and say "it's gonna be okay it's gonna be okay it's gonna be okay" over and over and over, and since that is just slightly less annoying than the screaming, I take control of the situation by ransacking the diaper bag, in hopes of finding something to stop the infernal sound that is coming out of her face-hole: Binky? Lambie? Superplus tampon hanging out of a torn wrapper? Nothing works. She just gets redder and louder.

I reach into the wall pocket and pull out a SkyMall magazine. Nothing thrills me more than the SkyMall. Where else can you buy a one-person submarine for only nine thousand dollars? But the child does not share my love for the Mall of the Sky; she just rips the magazine out of my hand and flings it—and the tampon—onto the lap of a businessman sitting two rows back.

The captain's voice comes over the loudspeaker, "Ladies and gentlemen, we cannot take off until *everyone*," he is clearly referring to me, "takes their seats."

As a last-ditch effort, I grab an air-sickness bag, draw a face on it, reach inside, and say the funniest thing I can think of: "Ooga booga."

The kid stops crying, then smiles, then *giggles*. "More puppet?" I ask. "MO PUPPA!" she says. The orange-level threat has been averted. Frau Stewardess smiles, blessing me with a nod. I couldn't be prouder if I'd just disarmed a hijacker with a Uniball pen and a lavender-scented sleep mask.

I think perhaps I should write a column in *Family Circle Magazine,* one in which I offer helpful parenting advice under headings like "Changing the World, One Diaper at a Time."

The child—now human again—interrupts my fantasy publishing life. "Mo Puppa, Momma!" I kiss her head, thank the gods above for blessing me with such natural parenting ability, then think to myself, "Sure, one puppet is fine, but two puppets—now *that's* a show!" I reach into the wall pocket in front of my husband's seat and take out his air-sickness bag. I draw a face, give it curly hair and glasses so that it looks like me—I know, nice touch—and stick my hand inside.

And then my world contracts.

Seems this air-sickness bag has been used before . . . but not for a puppet show. No, it's been used for the purpose that God intended. My husband looks at me, understanding immediately what has happened. He is horrified, though I think I see the tiniest hint of a smile creep across his face. After deciding to divorce him the minute we touch down, I turn to the matter at hand . . . on hand . . . IT'S ON MY HAND!!

You'd think that having a child has prepared you for the bodily functions of humanity, until you find yourself wearing a glove made of the puke of a stranger.

I spring out of my seat, afflicted digits still in bag.

Of course, there is no lavatory in the front of the plane, where we are, in the bulkhead seats. I curse my flirtation skills and then make my way to the bathroom in the back of the plane. But the aisle is filled with humans lumbering to their seats. I want to crawl between their legs, leapfrog over them, fatally stab the stewardess if I have to, whatever it takes to get to that bathroom.

Finally, I claw open the lavatory door and lock myself in. I take a deep breath, then pull out the hand.

It is covered in a substance that is thick, wet, viscous, and sprinkled with flecks of something—honey-roasted peanuts, perhaps?

As I scrub my hand in water hot enough to cause a third-degree burn, I think maybe I should save the bag for its DNA, just in case I acquire some rare, undefined flesh-eating disease and need to identify the mystery cookie tosser. But no, I'd rather go to my death than have to look into the face of the person whose guts I have touched.

Now clean, I take a moment to marvel at what has occurred: Roughly two million people fly the friendly American skies every day. How many of those travelers reach for, and then actually use, an air-sickness bag? And of those phantom pukers, how many would choose to put the vomit-filled vessel back into the seat pocket? And then, what's the probability that a cleaning crew would overlook this sack o' sick? Finally, what are the odds that all of this would become the perfect setup for one arrogant idiot who attempts to make a hand puppet out of a barf bag?!

Fuck Me.

As I leave the bathroom and make my way back to the (argh!) bulkhead seat, I stare into the faces of the last hurried stragglers boarding the plane. They look agitated, each one facing the prospect of a middle seat. "You think that's bad?" I want to say. "If that's the worst thing that happens to you today, then you, my friend, have hit the jackpot, because you're looking at a woman who has seen into the abyss." But I don't say that. Instead, I hurry back to my seat where the child is now sleeping, clutching the puke-free puke bag to her chest like a teddy bear. Normally, an event like this would send me into a rage, long enough to write at least half of an angry letter of complaint, but as I watch her sleep, my anger deflates. I will not condemn this Barfing Bandit, whose moment of lapsed judgment has made my arm's-length list of life's most disgusting experiences. Who am I to judge? If somebody filmed all of my questionable life moments and then edited them together, the resulting movie would be about three hours shorter than my actual life span. All I can do is chalk this one up to experience. Parenthood is a minefield of unpredictability: sometimes the mines are made of tears; sometimes they're made of undigested food.

Anyway, it's possible that the occurrence of this mathematical improbability has created a statistical vortex, one in which we are virtually guaranteed that this plane will land safely. So thank you, former passenger of seat 1B, wherever you are, for saving our lives with a single well-placed heave.

seven

PLAYDATE IN THE PARK: AN ODE

A day at the park, 'twas like any other
for a young(ish), sleep-deprived, bored-stiff new mother

I'd answered a Craigslist ad based in my 'hood
for a play group that sounded like it might be good.

"Bring yourself and your wee ones on down to the park
for a two-hour playdate; starts 10:00 a.m. sharp!"

We schlep to said spot, snack bag firmly in hand.
I plunk the kid down in the box of foul sand.

Then plop my own ass on a bench near the gate,
fix my hair, check my teeth, and await our play "dates"!

The playground gate opens, the first to appear
is a mom, her four kids, and two tons of kid gear.

She's a **Go-Getter Mom,** texting as she speaks.
She got more done this morning than I did this week.

She talks without stopping, can't get in a word.
I said my name twice, though there's no sign she heard.

In a minute come more folks, one cute little tot,
and with him his **Sexy Mom,** dressed weirdly hot.

In stilettos, a half top, and low low-rise jeans,
she "JUST GOT VAJAZZLED!" then shows
what that means.*

Next up comes a mom who smells like a bong.
She came with a friend, they're the **Party-Girl Moms.**

That one pours Kahlua through her Starbucks lid
while the other one keeps losing track of her kid.

I'm feeling uneasy, not to be a dick,
I'm thinking I'd like to get outta here. Quick.

But I can't leave just yet, my kid's having fun.
I'll stick it out twenty more minutes, then done.

From a sleek minivan **High-Achieving Mom** comes.
Her "Lean-In" success makes me feel like chewed gum.

She's got five under-fives, and has three PhD'ses
Why, just yesterday she cured three diseases!

Between her twin tots, spoken languages: nine.
It's clear their IQ's are much higher than mine.

---

*VAJAZZLING: the application of rhinestones and other gem stones around the vulvar area. See also: "SERIOUSLY?!"

Here comes **Neat Mom,** dressed in white ethereal,
dunking her kids in gel antibacterial.

Her sons are so spotless, such perfect grooming
for toddlers, it's hard to believe they're human.

More mommies arriving, good Lord they keep coming.
Each one less my speed, I'm increasingly bumming.

That's the **Shitty Kid Mom,** and oh, how I pity her,
cuz bad as her kids are, they'll only get shittier.

Her daughter's pure nasty, the kid's always scheming.
Her son's even worse, I think he's part demon.

There's **Sailor-Mouth Mom,** who in between fussing
with her newborn baby, just cannot stop cussing.

She's tossing out "f-ck" bombs and "sh-t" bombs away.
"C-sucker," "d-licker," "eff me in the A!"

Hippie Mom of patchouli she smells, to high heaven,
while breast-feeding her kids, ages nine and eleven.

As I scan the faces of this mommy throng,
it's totally clear to me, I don't belong.

I suppose I could flee, run fast as I can,
leave the child behind, in the cat box of sand.

But this problem extends past this day, and beyond.
Seems I've ruined my life giving birth. I've signed on

to a stream of mom friends to whom I can't relate.
S'pose I'll have to just suck it up, accept my fate.

When in walks a mom with a girl my kid's age.
She sits by herself; I decide to engage.

Her kid's not annoying, plays nice with my baby.
The mom seems quite normal, I start to think maybe

that this one's the **RIGHT MOM,** she's much
more my speed.
She's sarcastic and funny—she reminds me of me!

I have visions of lunches and weekend playdates
where we'll hang out and talk about moms who we hate!

I find myself feeling relieved and relaxed—
when she ups and excuses herself sorta fast.

She wrangles her kid, says she's late for a date,
and pushes her stroller right out of the gate.

I ask for her number; she says, "That's okay.
I've got plenty of 'mom' friends. Thanks anyway!"

And away she goes, without another word,
I must've looked shocked, like I'd eaten a turd.

A hand on my shoulder, I can't recall which,
with a voice that says, "HOLY SHIT, WHAT A BITCH!"

"FUCK HER!" says Sailor Mouth Mom. "AND
FUCK HER REJECTION.
"YOU'RE NOT HERE FOR JUDGMENT, OR
HER SEARCH FOR PERFECTION."

"A MOM'S DAY CAN BE SO FUUUUUCKING
MIND-NUMBING.
WE COME HERE FOR SUPPORT, AND TO BE
FUCKING WEL-COMING!"

Though Sailor Mouth Mom has an odd choice of phrases,
I am stung by her words, and the point that she raises.

So with her sage input, a new point of view,
and a vow to be less judge-y, I join the crew.

Cuz this is where ALL moms—me too—can belong.
So I introduce myself to the vajazzler.
And the chick with the bong.

eight

OH, YOU SHOULDN'T HAVE

It's late December and I've just squeezed a nine-pound girl child through my hoo-ha. She's being cleaned in the hospital nursery while her new, freaked-out father keeps watch. I am still in the delivery room, feeling exhausted, slightly throbbing, but mostly happy that it's over and I no longer feel like I am passing a solar flare through my lady parts.

My nurse, a sweet southern belle in pink floral scrubs, cleans up what looks like the aftermath of a murder. She is tossing bags of goo into a bin marked "human waste" or something equally demeaning.

On the counter sits a large plastic vat containing the placenta. Unless you've recently expelled one, you may be unaware that it is the organ responsible for nourishing the unborn child. Think of it like a bag lunch that lasts nine months. While some incense-burning individuals may charitably refer to its appearance as that of a flower or a "Tree of Life," I would suggest that it looks like something between a rotting jellyfish, a giant hydroencephalytic brain, or some unpronounceable Hungarian dish that contains way too much sauce, depending on the angle.

As I gaze upon this remarkable and repulsive bloated sack of slop, I become mesmerized by its glistening folds, and like a flesh-and-blood Rorschach it triggers in me thoughts of a friend, who for reasons that will become clear, I shall refer to only as "K."

We have been friends for a long time, K and I. She is a complex person; on the one hand, she's lovely, thoughtful, intelligent, and immensely successful in her professional endeavors; on the other, she is one of the most depraved people I have ever met, qualities upon which our deep friendship is based, qualities that led to the day when she put a petrified turd in a box, tied it up with a bow, and gave it to me as a joke.

And unlike her, I shit you not.

It was K's birthday, so when she handed me the beautifully wrapped gift, the only thing I could think of to say was, "But it's *your* birthday." I was shocked, of course. Disgusted, without a doubt. But mostly, I was impressed.*

---

*OKAY. LET ME JUST SAY THIS: We were very young when this happened. It was a period of high shenanigans. Also, K was an "artist." And it was the '90s. Now if she were to do this to me today, I can't guarantee that I wouldn't call the cops on her, or at the very least lose her phone number. But at the time, it was one of the strangest and most surprising incidents of my then young and way too easily impressed life.

And ever since that day, I have been hoping for an opportunity to exact my revenge.

And here it is, in Delivery Room 6B, staring me in the face, about to be tossed out like so many pounds of glop. I imagine how the deed will go down: I will hand K a hefty box tied with ribbon. She will look at it and say, "But *you're* the new mother . . . "

It will be sublime.

The conversation with my nurse goes something like this:

"Sooooo, that's the placenta, right?"

"Yes. It is."

"Can I have it?"

Long pause.

"Why?"

I consider telling her that I want to do what countless hippie pagans do with theirs: Boil it? Bake it? Bury it? Bathe in it? I don't know. But I can't lie to her. I feel that we have really bonded over the past few hours, and something in me wants to impress her. So I tell her my story. My poo-revenge story.

Wrong choice. Apparently, seeing a human being spring forth from my loins hasn't bonded her to me in the same way.

"I can't do that," she drawls. "I'd lose my job."

But I will not be kept down by the man, even if that man is a woman with a blonde ponytail in a blood-spattered nurse's uniform. I'm thirty-nine years old, God-damnit. I stand a better chance of getting dry-humped by

George Clooney during an autumn hayride than conceiving another child.

So I beg.

She stares at me with an expression that lives somewhere between contempt and fear.

"I am going to leave the room for a few minutes. What you do in that time is your own deal. I don't want to know anything about it."

And ten minutes later I am being transported to my private room in a wheelchair. On my face is one very wide grin, on my lap is one very large pillow, and below that is one very goopy, Tupperware-encased, contraband placenta.

When I arrive at my room, I hide the placenta-ware in a dark corner and settle in. My husband is sitting on the bed, cradling our new baby daughter. It is then that I remember why I'm here. Not to get even with my box-crapping friend. No, I am here to be with the brand-new human that my husband and I have created. So I turn my attention to my beautiful family. And for thirty-six hours the placenta sits in a plastic tub under a pile of blankets and luggage, doing God knows what. Rotting? Maybe. Creating another life? I don't know.

So when K calls the following day to announce that she will "be there in five minutes," I stumble around in a panic. I'm not ready! I haven't gift wrapped it! I should have refrigerated it! What if it stinks?! What if when she opens it, the smell is so offensive she screams and draws the attention of a passing ethics committee? . . .

I tell myself that it doesn't matter. This will be good. This will be *just*.

And then K walks into the room, and when she sees the new baby she begins to cry, I begin to cry, the baby begins to cry, and the whole thing is so moving I lose my nerve. Thirty minutes later K leaves with no knowledge of how close she'd come to being face-to-face with my insides.

Twenty-four hours later we are discharged. But I can't leave the evidence in the hospital—I gave Nurse Ratched my word. So it comes home with us, along with the baby, some balloons, and about fifty pairs of disposable panties.

And once we're home I can't throw it in the trash—it's human remains. I can't do that to my garbageman (though, evidently, I can't wait to do it to a close friend).

So into the freezer it goes. I tell myself that I will follow through with the plan. But the sad truth is that it falls down the priority list, somewhere under "keep new human alive" and "try to find a pair of pants that fits my now hamburger-shaped vagina."

Until my husband gets a new job and we are suddenly in the throes of moving from Los Angeles to Chicago.

Now I am in a bind, one that gives me a newfound respect for serial killers. You don't realize how hard it is to dispose of human organs until you've got one about to be evicted from its under-the-Häagen-Dazs hiding place.

I consider burying it in the yard. Not for hippie voo-doo reasons, just to get rid of the damn thing. But there's already an offer on our house, and I worry that the housing inspector will uncover the evidence, causing the buyers to back out on the basis that the house has been built on disturbingly fresh Indian burial ground.

Meanwhile, we finish packing. My husband leaves to drive the dog and his stamp collection across the country. I tuck the baby under one arm and the frozen entrée under another, and the three of us head out to spend our last night in town at a skeezy hotel by the airport.

That's when K calls, suggesting that we spend our last night at her house. She's out of the country, but her aunt Ellen is house-sitting and she won't mind.

Sweet Caroline, there is a God.

So off we go, into the belly of the beast! Well, into a very nice guest room . . . inside the belly of the beast!

I consider leaving the placenta-sicle in K's freezer, but after all this time that just feels lazy. Also, I don't want to chance her aunt thinking it's a tray of leftovers and trying to reheat it—that's a form of collateral damage that I'm just not willing to risk.

There is only one conceivable option: I must bury it in K's yard.

↜↝

Now it is the morning of our departure.

The baby is napping.

The cab will be here in twenty minutes.

It's now or never.

It's raining. Not wanting to endure a five-hour cross-country flight with soggy shoes, I take them off, then grab the thawing organ. I run outside in my bare feet, heading straight to K's gardening shed. I grab a shovel, and in the pouring rain I run down the old wooden staircase that leads to the garden. It is then that I lose my footing.

Up, into the air—I, the shovel, the placenta, we all go . . . slipping and sliding, down countless stairs, no shoes to stop me . . . As I watch the shovel spin in the air above my head, it occurs to me that I may die in the next moment. I will have made it through childbirth only to be killed by the placenta almost nine months later . . . and wouldn't that be ironic.

The shovel comes down on top of my leg, leaving me with a three-inch gash. I am alive. Bleeding, in pain, and laughing hysterically, but alive.

I continue down the stairs, limping toward the back fence, where I find a small, Charlie Brown–looking shrub, under which I dig a hole. I plop the big, bloody ice cube into the hole and then bury it. I give it a couple of solid pats and say a small prayer that Aunt Ellen's Chihuahua, "Mister Pants," doesn't dig it up. Battered and bruised, I pump a halfhearted victory fist into the air and run back up to the house.

Aunt Ellen is standing on the back deck, holding a cup of coffee. She is staring at me.

I am dripping wet, bare feet caked in mud, blood streaming down my leg. I am holding a shovel. There is no question that I look like a careless and slovenly murderer.

I can hear the cab honking in the driveway. And though there is no time for it, I tell Aunt Ellen that I've just buried a placenta in her niece's yard.

She smiles. "How sweet. You planted fertility in her garden!"

My jaw tightens. She's absolutely right. If you believe in that crap—which K does—that's exactly what I've done. Not only have I not gotten my revenge, I've essentially provided K with the hippie-voodoo means to produce a child, including a placenta that will one day most certainly find itself in my hands—or, knowing K, in my digestive tract, courtesy of a plate of home-cooked plasagna.

So here I am, back at square one of my poo-revenge plot. I'm thinking now that it's time I took a simpler "eye for an eye" approach. My birthday is in October. Until then, I'll be stocking up on gift boxes and eating plenty of roughage.

nine

FIGHT THE PINK

Back when I was newly pregnant, sometime during the first trimester we found ourselves at the OB's office for a routine ultrasound to determine that the kid was healthy and to find out what it was going to be.[*]

Some people like to save this knowledge to be revealed as a surprise the moment the baby is born. Personally, I can't stand the idea of someone possessing information about me to which I am not privy. Though it does give me the opportunity to use the word *privy*, it generally feels to me like the first step of a blackmail plot. And while I'm certain that I could have kept the secret from the husband if he'd insisted on waiting, there's no way I'd have been

---

[*]I.e., Gender-wise; species-wise we were pretty clear on what to expect.

able to keep from taunting him mercilessly and holding that knowledge over his head, which I'm guessing is probably not the optimal environment in which to bring a child into the world.

Fortunately, he felt the same way I did; neither of us could understand why anyone would need to save the surprise for the delivery room. Aren't there enough surprises, between "Guess how much college is going to cost in eighteen years?" to "Whoa, Nelly! I think I just gave birth to a Conehead." But, as I like to say, each to his own.*

After I lay down on the examination table, Dr. V. Jay lathered up my pooch-y tummy with KY Jelly and began peering through my guts.

Swooping the ultrasound paddle over my belly as though it were an air-hockey table—a flabby, bloated air-hockey table—the doc directed our attention to the monitor, on which he pointed out the baby's head and facial features, the spine, and some tendrils that would apparently become arms and legs, all of which looked more like a thermal weather map than a human to me. Then, with all the drama of a game-show host, he said, "Let me ask you one more time: are you sure you want to know the sex of this baby?"

The husband and I looked at each other.

"Uh, yeah," I said.

"So you *do* want me to tell you," said the doctor.

"Yes," I said.

---

*A phrase I like to use when talking about people whose opposing beliefs are both (a) different from mine and (b) 100 percent wrong.

"You're sure about that?" he asked again.

"Yes!" I said, feeling agitated and certain that my fear of blackmail plots was about to be validated; either that or we were about to win the Showcase Showdown.

The doctor pointed to the low-pressure front on the ultrasound screen and said, "There's one lip, and there's the other lip. It's a girl!" My husband looked at me, confused, and asked, "He can tell that from her face"? To which I responded quietly, "I don't think he's talking about the lips up top."*

Once we'd both taken a moment to get past the doctor's strangely porn-y choice of words, the husband pumped a fist in the air and shouted, "YES!"

Me, not so much.

↜↝

The husband was confused by my lukewarm, less-than-overjoyed response to the news that we were having a girl.

Certainly, a big chunk of my disappointment was the loss of possibility. I've always loved those life moments of infinite potential—like when you get something in the mail from the gas company and your first thought is "Maybe there's a check for five thousand dollars in there!" followed by the next thought, "Or maybe it's awkward nude photos of me taken from inside our bathroom heating vent." It's why it takes me forever

---

*I still can't explain why he used the terminology of *Hustler* magazine, but I'm just going to stick with the assumption that he thought we were cool enough to handle it.

to choose from a list of thirty-nine flavors and why I die just a little after saying, "I'll have the chocolate." There's something so delicious about that sweet spot of unlimited possibility. And learning that we were having a girl meant closing the door on a lifetime of unique, mom-to-a-boy experiences that I wouldn't get to savor, like being my son's first "special lady" and the privilege of making life for every subsequent "special lady" in my son's life a living hell.

I'd assumed we were having a boy, for a number of very good reasons. There aren't many females in our lineages; I have two brothers, and my husband has one brother. Also, my friend Pete (who also has a brother) had dangled his wife's wedding ring over my belly during a backyard kegger, and when the ring swung back and forth in a straight line, Pete had drunkenly proclaimed it a boy.

Between all that hard science, I was certain there was a tiny penis up in there.

Of course, I'd been spewing that old hairy chestnut, "It doesn't matter what it is, as long as it's *healthy*," right up until the moment that we heard it was indeed going to be a lip-tastic girl. But the deep truth is that I wasn't just assuming it was a boy; I'd been hoping for one.

Certainly, there are things about little boys that I've never quite understood—like the way they mindlessly yank on their penises as though they're made of Silly Putty. Still, despite my own lip-having status, I've always related to boys better than girls,* and the fact is, I didn't know

---

*Fact: I am known in some circles as a Manly Lady.

much about the care, feeding, and raising of a girl. Maybe it has something to do with my upbringing,* maybe not.

Regardless, once we learned that there would be no tiny penis-tugging in our immediate futures, my feelings about raising a girl human progressed fairly quickly, from confusion to ambivalence to fear to sleepiness to a powerful sense of duty, which is where it stuck. If I couldn't raise a boy who would grow to appreciate a nontraditional Manly Lady like myself—then, by golly, I would do the next best thing and raise a Manly Lady-Girl.

So while other mothers-to-be (and at least one particular father-to-be) cry in delight at the prospect of their precious, dainty little girls-to-be, I went in, shall we say, a different direction. Not so far as that Canadian couple who named their baby "Envelope" and attempted to raise her/him entirely gender-free . . . but probably further than most, when I established "Operation Fight the Pink."

(Although I did not keep a formal record of the events that ensued, what follows is a reasonable facsimile, using old e-mails, text messages, conversations with my husband, and random bits of paper stuck at the bottom of my purse.)

OPERATION FIGHT THE PINK

Be it resolved that on this, the day of our daughter's birth, I am putting my gnarled foot down, and, with all due respect to the husband (who is, let the record show, shaking his head right now), I hereby decree the following feminist goals for my child.

---

*Please see Appendix A.

1. My daughter will not be "defined" by the color pink. (This is in reference to clothing, toys, and accessories, less so to naturally occurring food items and her own body parts. Those are permitted to remain pink.) If I've learned one thing in all those women's studies classes—well, that one I took in my first year of college—it is that pink is the color of oppression and tyranny. And Mary Kay cosmetics.

2. She will be exposed to gender-neutral activities (soccer, karate, electric guitar lessons, WWE wrestling) over female-oriented activities (ballet, needlepoint, harpsichord lessons, *So You Think You Can Dance*).

3. She will never, under any circumstances, be allowed to dress up like a princess (Disney trademarked or otherwise). Ever. Possible exception: Princess Leia. (Exception to the exception: space bikini. That will *not* fly here.)

4. My child will be a survivor—I don't just mean metaphorically; she must be able to handle herself in an apocalypse (zombie or otherwise). This means that when fully grown, she must be strong enough to carry me (anywhere between 130–200 pounds; I will do my best to keep it on the low end, but you know . . . metabolism) and demonstrate a basic understanding of electricity, chemistry, several martial arts, weapons handling, and some emergency medical training. She must also know how to use a chain saw.

I feel confident that, in adhering to these guidelines, our daughter will not follow in the dainty footsteps of countless girls before her who have mindlessly welcomed the pink shackles of lady-hood, but instead will be her own person—a self-sufficient, self-respecting, powerful member of society. With zombie-ass-kicking abilities.

Eight Months In

Operation Fight the Pink is fully under way, though it has not been without its challenges.

It has been difficult to enforce the "no pink" rule. Throughout the year we received many gifts for the baby, and while I am grateful for the generosity of our friends and family, 85 percent of the gifts fell somewhere on the pink spectrum from "light cherry blossom" to "neon hot 'n slutty." It seems we are stuck with said gifts, as attempting to return them seems impractical and time-consuming; also, the husband got very pissed when I even suggested this (that sappy bastard).

Regarding gender-biased activities, it may be too soon to tell, but based on her affinity for the Jolly Jumper, I think she may have a talent for basketball (coed).

On the subject of princessification—we may have some work ahead of us; while at a birthday party she reached for a princess tiara with flashing lights. I intercepted said tiara and handed her a building block instead. When the child became agitated I attempted to demonstrate how much fun a rectangular piece of wood can be. A screaming tantrum ensued. So as not to ruin the party, I allowed a compromise: I let the child wear the block on her head. Success (?).

Two Years–ish

OFTP is not going so well.

Pink continues to dominate the color palette in our home. I tried to remove all the pink crayons from her crayon box, only to find that the child had been hoarding—and eating—them. (Her diapers have been a daily reminder of my failure in this regard.)

Took child to the park to watch a peewee baseball game. She was eager, but quickly lost interest after consuming one hot dog, a bucket of popcorn, and two ice cream bars. We lost more ground when she was invited to run the bases after the game—which she declined in favor of chasing a butterfly into the outfield.

If she absolutely has to be interested in princesses—and it appears by her unwavering tiara obsession that she does—I am praying that they at least be the tougher, less pansy-assed ones, like Mulan. Just please, *not* Cinderella, the lamest of the princesses, who waits helplessly for some fancy-britches-wearing prince who uses far too much hair gel and who "saves" her by identifying her tiny shoe size, which I'm guessing is simply evidence that her feet had been bound.

In addition to the foregoing, a troubling development has arisen.

While at the grocery store the other day, an elderly man stopped to tell me that my daughter was "very pretty." I said, "Okay," and continued sniffing a piece of raw chicken. The man went on, "Really. She is so cute!" "Okay then," I said and started to walk away. The man continued, "Really . . . ," to the point that I nearly shoved the old geezer into the frozen shrimp section.

The fact is: sure, she's "cute." She's got that blonde-haired, blue-eyed, leggy thing going on that our society seems to like so much. And as humans go, yes, her features are organized in a symmetrical configuration that one might call attractive. Me, I call it disastrous. It's not that I'm jealous (though it is a fact that the highest compliment I was ever paid as a child was, "You would have made a really good-looking boy"). What irks me is that, just by virtue of being a girl, she will face constant evaluation on the basis of her looks.[*] I was really counting on her being homely—but things are not looking good, as it appears she may, in fact, be good-looking. Fingers crossed that I'm wrong.

THREE YEARS, ONE MONTH

She wore a tutu for five straight days, at which point it started to smell like an old, rotting fish net. And then I

---

[*] Look, I've heard about all those studies linking physical attractiveness to professional success, and if she can sail through life on her looks, then I guess that bodes well for my husband and me and the quality of retirement home that she'll eventually stick us into. But for the sake of her humanity, I'd still rather she were a little more nerdy/awkward/homely/dorky. Not just because all of those words have described me at one time or another (also now), but because I've heard it straight from the mouths of "babes" (i.e., the grown-lady kind) that their striking good looks often make life more—not less—difficult (i.e., problems with female friendships, men feeling intimidated by them, the world not taking them seriously). This being so, two rhetorical questions: (1) Is it too much to hope that my child could learn to get along in life solely on her personality, intelligence, and pluck? And (2) would I be going too far in considering physically disfiguring her? Just wondering.

caught her wearing my bra. True, she was wearing it on her head, but I attribute this to her poor hand-eye coordination more than anything else.

Also, the child has become obsessed with wearing makeup. I have tried to express to her that, for me, makeup is primarily for spackling purposes, but this has not swayed her from habitually attempting to paint her face like some two-bit, pull-up-wearing floozy.

When we moved a few months ago, the husband insisted that the child be allowed input into redecorating her room. As a result, her bedroom now has pink walls, pink sheets, and a pink light fixture. It looks like someone ground up a bunch of flamingos into a paste and flung it on her walls.

Today she asked me if she looks cute when she's sleeping. My immediate, unedited response, "No. You're hideous." It didn't hurt her feelings—on the contrary, she simply chose not to believe me. So, on a positive note, her self-esteem is rock solid. On the other hand: GROSS.

Four Years and Change

On Halloween it really seemed as though we were making progress. Though she'd asked to be Cinderella for her preschool Halloween party (ugh), she also expressed a desire to go trick-or-treating as Spider-Man (yay!). This was a decided win, though in retrospect, perhaps I shouldn't have shouted, "HELL, YEAH!!!!"

I made my way to the mall, where I found a top-notch Spider-Man costume, the last one at the store. Another mother tried to wrest it from my hands, but I wasn't about to give it up. She even made her son ask me for it (seriously, lady, how desperate can you be, shoving your crying kid at me?), but I think the experience will serve him well—he should learn that life is filled with disappointment.

When I awoke on Halloween morning, the kid was already dressed in a homemade Cinderella outfit she'd cobbled together (blue towel, dishwashing gloves, tinfoil crown, and "magic toilet paper wand"). Unnerved, I held out the Spider-Man outfit, but she shook her head and said she'd "changed her mind." I bit my tongue and let her wear the damn princess outfit to preschool. It was later, when she got home from school and refused to change into her Spider-Man costume for the evening's festivities, that I may have lost my cool. I won't divulge exactly what went down, except to say that strong words were spoken, tears were released, and a twenty-minute time-out was given (to me; by me).

All of which is to explain how I found myself, the following morning, filled with a form of regret that can be purged only by driving to the mall and purchasing a fully licensed Cinderella costume, complete with a real fake wand and Lucite slippers. Yes, it was a hard pill to swallow, but at least the gown is blue. The look on the kid's face when I gave it to her—that did help the pill go down. And the 25 percent off post-Halloween discount—that paid for the pill.

CONCLUSION

Despite my attempts to mold the girl in my Manly Lady image, it seems that it is not to be. She's proven herself to be a Barbie-playing, jewelry-loving pretty pink princess, a fact that baffles me, as all I've ever wanted is for her to be her own woman (unless that woman is a Barbie-playing, jewelry-loving pretty pink princess). So rather than impose my will on her—as righteous and correct as I still believe it to be—I have chosen to stand down and abandon OFTP, and instead will look upon this as a "learning experience": she may be my daughter—but in the end, she's her own person.

We all have dreams for our kids, until the day we discover that their dreams are not ours to have. And though you may pray that your daughter becomes a judo–black belt, multilingual engineering student at Yale, she just may end up the second-highest-paid stripper at "Cheeks' Bar and Grill." And I guess, as long as she's happy, there's nothing wrong with that.* † ‡

---

*As long as she's your kid.

† (Just kidding.)

‡ (No, I'm not.)

ten

MY BODIES, MYSELF

S he woke up screaming "STEEZIN DA QUOZIT! STEEZIN DA QUOZIT!" After a few minutes of rocking and snot wrangling, I was able to get to the root of it. She'd had a nightmare about Steve. The guy from *Blues Clues*. She thought he was hiding in her closet.

This brought me great joy.

Now, it's true that I have always been attracted to "Steve"—the host of this mind-numbing Nickelodeon show—to the point that (a) I did place an eBay bid on, and after a hair-raising bidding war did win, the entire series of *Blues Clues* on DVD, and then (b) summarily discarded the single disc containing the episodes hosted by Steve's replacement, "Joe," whose round face and lack of charisma make me want to punch something.

But the pleasure I felt after my three-year-old's first night terror had nothing to do with Steve, my not-so-secret future second husband.

It was all about her and me.

Until that moment I'd had no sense that she shared any of my genetic material, despite the fact that she was conceived inside my body and did, indeed, shoot out of my loins like a cannonball.

Back when she was growing in my belly, I'd imagine the little girl she'd become. In my wildest fantasies she was somewhere between *Little Miss Sunshine* and that kid from *Welcome to the Dollhouse:* a chubby, nerdy, socially awkward little dork. Sometimes I'd toss in a little deformity, like a clubfoot, a lazy eye, or a third nipple growing out of her face. She would be my Beautiful Little Underdog™.

Instead, I gave birth to a Disney princess who looks like we stole her from a pair of privileged and well-adjusted Swedish downhill skiers.

I am on the short side with a laugh like a pellet gun and a head full of frizzy hair that looks like something a cat threw up. And while I find my husband attractive, he frequently describes his appearance as that of a thumb. Our daughter, on the other hand, is gorgeous and girl-ish, with almond-shaped blue eyes, silky blonde hair, and long, willowy legs that come up to my Adam's apple. If I hadn't witnessed with my own two eyes the sight of her punching her way out of my vagina like some character in a Quentin Tarantino movie, I wouldn't have believed she was ours . . . or, more specifically, *mine*.

But that night, after seeing her in the throes of boogey-man terror, I began to see that perhaps she is a bit more like me than I thought.

✦

My first boogeyman's name was Norman, and he hid under my bed. I can't take credit for inventing him—he was not so loosely based on a friend of the family, a mild-mannered tax attorney with long, slender hands. It may sound silly, but trust me: when you're four years old, the specter of a grown man preparing tax returns under your bed while you sleep is terrifying.

After my parents took me to see *Night of the Living Dead*—when I was *seven* (note to self: check statute of limitations with Child Protective Services)—Norman the Boogeyman evolved into a never-ending slew of random dead guys. And the under-my-bed part was replaced by *the whole world*. That pile of leaves? A cover for a rotting cadaver. That upright freezer by the side of the road? Filled with bodies chopped up and stacked like logs. Attics, closets, crawl spaces, porta-potties—all were fair game for my corpse-based fears.

Perhaps this is where my daughter and I diverge?

Perhaps not.

✦

The kid is in her little girly room, diligently focused on drawing a picture. "What's that?" I ask. "Is that a kitty and a doggy hugging?"

"NO," she says. "IT'S TWO VAMPIRES. THEY'RE EATING EACH OTHER. SEE? THAT'S THE BLOOD!"

My immediate instinct is to correct her and point out that she's way off base with this one: vampires are not the same as zombies—they don't eat flesh; they suck blood. Everybody knows that—it's a pretty basic distinction. And even if they did eat flesh, how could they eat each other simultaneously? It doesn't even make sense. Then I remember—she's only three. Such subtleties would only be lost on her. Instead, I praise her for how well she's coloring inside the lines.

~~~

I grew up in Winnipeg, which is a Cree word meaning "Mucky Waters," in a house on the banks of the Red River, the very mucky waters for which the city was named.

Friends were in short supply the summer after seventh grade. I was no longer speaking with Theresa Spak, not since she'd disputed my claim that I'd invented the euphemisms "Number One" and "Number Two" for discussing bodily functions. "*Somebody* invented it. Why is it so hard to believe it was me?" I'd screamed over mayonnaise sandwiches. (Years later I would come to realize that I was wrong, but by then there was too much Number One under the bridge to do anything about it.)

Then there was Elena Hrabiuk, a girl I'd met at orchestra camp. Elena had wide-set eyes and usually smelled of fried pierogi. Seeing that my only alternative was to spend the afternoon with my brother Aaron while he belched "This Land Is Your Land" at my face, I called Elena and invited her over.

We hung out in my room for forty-five minutes or so, crying to the greatest hits of Air Supply. After the batteries in my boom box died, we went out to the backyard, where my dad was standing over the barbecue, swearing at a plate of raw hamburger. My dad was once a radical hippie, and back in the day he had marched at Berkeley, but now he was living on the Canadian prairies and the only remnants of his hippie past were the three hits of acid chilling in the refrigerator crisper. He suggested we "go play down by the river." Since Elena was raised in eastern Europe and unfamiliar with the concept of sarcasm, she led the way.

We climbed down the bank through the slimy grass and muck and jumped onto our neighbor's dock.

The *Paddlewheel Queen* chugged past for its daily afternoon cruise. We jumped up and down, waving and yelling obscenities at the boat whose passengers consisted of a few drunken old ladies and some handicapped kids from a nearby group home. The boat sent a ripple of waves toward the dock, disturbing the dark water. My eye caught something floating, maybe fifty feet out. I picked up a rock and threw it at the object, nailing it.[*]

The object pitched and bobbed slowly with the weight of something dense.

I decided instantly that it was a human head.

I opened my mouth to call for my father, then stopped. Instinctively, I knew that this would go over like a lead turd due to my reputation as "The Little Girl Who Cried Corpse."

---

[*]Which is odd for me, since I throw like a girl with no arms.

I looked again. There was no way I was imagining this one. That floating head was so obviously the real deal, it made all my other dead-body hunches seem like the ramblings of a madwoman.

I yelled for him. "Dad!"

No answer.

I called again. "Dad!"

Finally, a response. "Fuck off, I'm cooking!"

Elena looked confused—there was no time to explain to her the intricacies of my family, or the fact that my father was likely stoned at that very moment. She took off in the direction of her house while I ran up the grassy slope, up to the barbecue, where my father was attempting to swat a bug with a greasy spatula.

I spoke carefully, "Dad, I need to show you something. We—I . . . I found a head."

A tiny piece of hamburger flew off his fly-swatting spatula and hit me in the cheek. I gave him a serious look, the kind I'd seen Lucy Ewing give J. R. numerous times.

"Dad. Please."

"Oh, for chrissake—all right, let's go."

I led him down to the dock and pointed to the bobbing head in the water.

My dad squinted at it. "That? It's just a piece of driftwood. Probably upturned by that fascist with the speedboat." I begged him to look again.

My dad considered it. "I guess I could call the River Patrol. It'll give me a chance to register a complaint about that fascist bastard."

He called, and in twenty minutes two mustachioed officers pulled up in a motorboat. I waved frantically, pointing to the spot where my detached head was bobbing. Mustache Number One drove the boat, circling around my soon-to-be-validated discovery. Mustache Number Two lowered a length of rope into the murky sludge and then, hand over hand, pulled the rope back into the boat.

On the end of the rope was not a head, but an entire friggin body.

I held my breath while they lifted the old man's corpse into the boat and then drove it over to the dock, where they laid him out. Pressing every wrinkly crease of my brain into service, I recorded the details of the unfolding event: The red-and-white-plaid shirt. The bald head that held a few soggy wisps, just above each ear. The brown leather shoe and leg brace on the right foot, and the shoeless black sock on the left.

One of the officers pulled a wallet from the dead guy's pocket. He opened it and retrieved a water-logged driver's license that showed an address just three blocks away. I caught sight of a huge wad of cash, possibly as much as twenty dollars, then wondered if my "finder's keepers" status would be legally binding when it came to claiming the money.

A couple of houses over was a tiny strip of public land where they found a cane and some muddy footprints at the river's edge. "Looks like he just fell in, eh?" said Mustache Number Two. As his partner radioed a call back to the precinct, my family started back up to the house to eat dinner. I was stunned. "How can you eat? There's a dead man in our yard!" My dad shrugged. "Ask him what he wants on his burger," he said as he walked up the steps and then pulled the sliding screen door shut behind him.

I stayed with the River Patrol until two more official-looking men with mustaches showed up, put the body onto a stretcher, and carried it to a plain white van in our driveway.

As the van pulled away I sat on the curb and pondered my future. Surely, I'd be getting a call from the police for my minute-by-minute eyewitness account of the whole body-finding event. Then I'd probably hear from Sylvia Kuzyk, the anchor lady from CKY-TV, with a request for an interview. I ran my fingers through my hair and silently cursed my mother for not letting me get my ears pierced now that I was going to be famous.

Sylvia didn't call. The police didn't call. Nobody called.

But that was okay. I didn't need their public recognition. I had something better and more lasting: sweet vindication. I wasn't weird for thinking dead bodies were everywhere. Turns out I was right all along.

～

So back to my Steve-fearing toddler. Maybe it was a one-time deal. Maybe a nightmare about a sexy, balding children's TV host is just that: a nightmare about a sexy, balding children's TV host. And yeah, maybe it's premature to be connecting the dots from a three-year-old's vision of a Nickelodeon television star with oddly sensual sloping shoulders to a lifetime of searching for corpses.

Or maybe it's a *sign*. A sign that she carries my gene. The body-finding one.

And maybe that's all she inherited from me. She may not share the disturbingly long, three-knuckled second toe that I possess, or my irrational fear of pigeons, but these differences don't make me love her any less. I can promise one thing: when she says, "Mom, I think there's a face staring up at me from the toilet," she's going to find me standing by her side with an understanding ear. And a camera, just in case she's right. Because it's a big world out there, and it's filled with corpses. And they're not going to find themselves. They need us, my daughter and me.

eleven

TWENTY-NINE THINGS I HAVE LOST SINCE BECOMING A PARENT

1. **Nipples that point in the same direction.**
2. **Bladder control** when I sneeze, laugh, do jumping jacks, or stand up from a seated position.
3. **The desire to party,** unless said partying involves lying on a couch watching old episodes of *Hart to Hart* while spraying a can of Redi-Whip into my mouth in short, steady bursts.
4. **The nail on my big toe,** after angrily kicking a semifunctional Diaper Genie and telling it (unironically) to "EAT SHIT!"
5. **My memory** of the last time my bras were washed. (Nearest estimate, spring 2011.)

6. **The ability to stay awake in a movie theater.** Or while watching a TV show after six o'clock. Or while reading an e-mail. Or right now . . .

7. **My virginity.** (Just making sure at least one of us is paying attention.)

8. **The capacity to wake up at 5 a.m. to go for a jog.**

9. **All credibility for implying that there was ever a time that I woke up at 5 a.m. to go for a jog.**

10. **The combination to locker 623** at the gym that I have been paying forty-five dollars a month since November 2007 to use, but which I have not actually set foot inside since March 2008.

11. **The notion that babies are pure, innocent, loving souls,** replaced by the knowledge that they are the neediest, most narcissistic creatures in the universe.*

12. **Patience for the sound of children whining,** after one minute.

13. **Patience for the sound of adults whining,** after twenty seconds.

14. **My crush on my ob-gyn** ever since the day that I looked between my legs and saw him one elbow deep inside me, the other arm holding a cell phone to his ear telling his wife that he may

---

*With the exception of a boss I once had whose ability to turn every conversation back to her was so amazing, upon reflection it may have been a superpower.

be late for dinner but that he would almost certainly be able to make the 8:00 show.

15. Since laying spread-eagle on a gurney in the hallway of a maternity ward, **the concern that someone might see my naked body.** (Now I couldn't care less if someone were to post in Times Square a high-def fifty-foot nude photo of me popping a chest pimple.)

16. **The beeper number to my pot dealer.**

17. **My badass rep.**

18. **Okay, I never actually had a badass rep. Or a pot dealer, for that matter.**

19. **The job that I interviewed for when I was eight months pregnant,** and after the interviewer asked, "Aren't you due to have a baby next month?" I said, "Yeah, I'll probably lay low for a coupla weeks afterward, but I should be ready to get back to work after two, three weeks, tops."

20. **My shit,** just now, upon rereading #19.

21. **A handle on current events;** if pop culture knowledge was an animal, mine would resemble a groundhog emerging every six weeks to randomly yell out a social trend ("Gangnam Style!" *"Game of Thrones*!" "Ryan Gosling!") only to retreat back into its hole of social oblivion and stale macaroni for another six weeks.

22. **My belief that children can be "molded"** into anything other than who they intrinsically are.

23. **An argument** with another new mom—a close friend—over the use of baby leashes.

24. **My friendship** with that mom.

25. **The ability to enjoy any form of entertainment in which a child is in danger,** even though when I was a kid I couldn't get enough of it and when *Flowers in the Attic* came out my friends and I passed that dog-eared paperback around the fourth grade like it was a *Playboy* and hoped/wished/prayed that someone would lock us in their crawl space, and when no one did, we all wondered what was wrong with us.

26. **A lifelong family friend** to a heart attack—a decidedly unfunny event.

27. **The illusion that anything in life is guaranteed.**

28. **The capacity to dwell on emotionally painful topics.**

29. **The hard shell around my heart,** causing me to weep openly at the beauty of life as it manifests in such moments as an elderly couple holding hands, a plastic bag blowing in the wind, or a pair of feral cats copulating in my backyard.

twelve

ALL THE BOYS I'VE LOVED BEFORE (YOUR DAD)

Just minutes after my friend's wedding ceremony, the three-year-old's face screws up into a grimace, and she begins to sob.

I ask her why she's crying.

"I WANNA GET MAWWIED!"

I am startled by her outburst, but more than that I am entertained, which, due to the fact that I am a horrible person, is often the effect that my daughter's emotional breakdowns have on me.

Until I hear her response to the groom's line of questioning.

"You're upset because you wanted to get married?" he asks.

She sobs heavily. "Y—Y—YETHHHHHH!"

"Who do you want to marry?" he asks.

"I WANN . . . I WANN . . . I WANNA MAWWY . . . MOMMY!"

And that's when she throws her chubby arms around my thighs, and I don't even care that she's getting snot and tears on my three-hundred-dollar silk bridesmaid's dress/future throw pillows. I just stand there, enjoying this sweet spot of parenthood, and the aroma of the deep-fried, bacon-wrapped hors d'oeuvres now being circulated on platters all around us only enhances the delicious perfection of the moment.

But while I am weirdly flattered by her proposal, it occurs to me that one day she's going to realize that she probably won't be marrying me (at least not until the laws around here change pretty drastically), and someday after that, she's going to throw her arms around some guy or girl the way she's hugging me now.

That's the day that consumes me. That day, and every day that comes after.

↝

My own dating history is a dark and meandering story filled with adventure, danger, lots of smeared mascara, and naughty bits in various states of undress. And ever since the day that my own child proposed marriage to me, I have been filled with a need to tell her the entire story: the story of all the men I've loved before.

But of course I can't, because she's barely out of diapers. At best it would just confuse her, and at worst I'd get picked up by Child Protective Services and locked up for being a pervert, because I'm guessing it's not appropriate to tell your toddler about the first time you got French-kissed by someone, especially since it wasn't her dad.

But what if I never get the chance? What if I drop dead from some all-over body tumor that I'll develop from standing too close to the microwave? How will I teach her what I learned about life from playing Strip Backgammon with my upstairs neighbor?

And if I live through Cancer of the Everything, even if I wait until she's of an appropriate age (twelve? fifteen? twenty-one? sixty-five?) to talk to her about it, there's a high probability that she'll hatemyfrigginguts (mother-hating being a mandatory rite of passage) and won't want to hear it from me, the way that I didn't want to hear it from my mom.*

And even then, if by some bizarre twist of nature she *doesn't* hatemyfrigginguts, I'll still be screwed because by that point, I'll be wearing sweater sets and pearls and suffering from a selective-memory syndrome that causes me to replace my personal history with the plot points of *Grease* (the sequel).

The only solution is this: I must write down deliberately and with absolute and horrifying clarity the story

---

*Who, while driving me to the library when I was fourteen years old, stopped at a red light and gave me the only piece of sexual advice she would give me: "Jojo," she said, "don't be flattered if a boy gets an erection," at which point I suddenly and spontaneously went blind.

of my former loves, and the lessons that they taught me, all while the memories and shame are still fresh enough to make me hot-faced and queasy. Because if she's anything like me (and considering the fact that we both love peanut butter, fart jokes, and watching ourselves cry in the mirror, it appears there is some significant overlap), this transcript may help guide her in her own future, and hopefully/possibly/dear-God-please help her avoid just a few of the XXXL-size mistakes I made.[*]

⤳

First I will tell her about **"Soccer Legs McGee,"**[†] the most beautiful high school boy who has ever existed in the history of formal education. His very presence in a room electrified me; it was as though he was the scent of a chocolate fountain, and I was a walking nostril, so attracted to him was I. He was a jock with a bad-boy streak; he loved heavy metal music and often threw parties where there were drinking and drugs, and if you were a girl you stood a very good chance of being felt up. Me, I played cello in the orchestra, owned all the greatest hits of Lionel Richie, and wouldn't have my first hit of pot until my twenties (and even then it would take four tries to get it right). Yet I had no shame where S. L. McGee was concerned; I sang

---

[*]I shall refer to romantic male-female relationships because those are the only ones with which I have personal experience; I've never dated a woman (though I do enjoy the music of k.d. lang), but if I had, you can be certain that I'd be spewing my half-baked theories about that too. In any case, I'm guessing the lessons are pretty much inter-gender-changeable.

[†]Names and details have been changed to protect the innocent, the douchebaggy, and that one guy who still lives in the blue house at 78 Atlantic Avenue.

songs to him in public, gave him unrequited gifts of over-sized stuffed animals, and publicly confessed my love to him with a regularity that causes me to thank the heavens hourly that Facebook didn't exist back then.

Surprisingly, my methods worked. It took a few years, but eventually I won him over and was able to call myself the official girlfriend of Soccer Legs McGee.

Soccer Legs McGee taught me **Lesson 1,** that, given enough ingenuity and lack of shame, **there is no person, place, thing, or goal that is out of your league or beyond your reach.**

I would learn the second lesson shortly thereafter, upon discovering that SLMcG and I were a poor match, due to the fact that (a) he hated books—all books—with a dumb passion, and (b) he loved making out with girls who were my locker partner.

Lesson 2, then, is that "Contents Are Not Always As Advertised," or, more specifically, **that personality, integrity, and intelligence bear positively no relation to muscular legs or the ability to grow a mustache in tenth grade.**

The next lesson came courtesy of "**The Slightly Older Man,**" the nineteen-year-old love of my seventeen-year-old life. He was the first guy who thought I was interesting and wanted to kiss me anyway. He was Nor-wegian, Spanish, and Korean, which made him tall, dark, and hairless. We dated for three months, until one evening when he said he was uncomfortable with our age difference and then drove away with my heart in the trunk of his Reliant K-Car. It was my first heartbreak, and it took me an embarrassingly long time to get over (i.e., several Olympics). But when I did, I learned **Lesson 3,** that, contrary to popular belief, **heartbreak is not fatal;** in fact, it's a necessity of modern life, for if not for heartbreak, (a) there would be no soft rock, (b) telephone psychics would be unemployed, and (c) waterproof mascara would never have been invented. I also learned that Sara Lee Cake tastes best when mixed with salty tears.

There was "**The Cherry Picker,**" who taught me the significance of my virginity, right around the time he left with it. (Can there ever be a perfect virginity-losing experience? Probably not. Studies show that 92 percent of Big V–losing experiences are awkward, uncomfortable, and involve the music of Spandau Ballet.) I'd never bought into the idea that one's virginity should be put on a pedestal like some kind of holy grail. As a young liberated woman, I found the idea offensive, archaic, and even a little dangerous. Yet the memory of that afternoon has since been rendered in high-def, 3-D detail with particular clarity on the moment that I looked into his eyes and realized that I would always remember it and what an enormous drag that was going to be. That was **Lesson 4,** that the worth of most "first" events in life—like the "losing" of one's so-called virginity—lies in how they translate into memory and that **a little consideration on behalf of your future self can save you from a lifetime of forehead-slapping regret.**

Lesson 5 came courtesy of "**Mr. Seemed Like a Good Idea at the Time,**" who taught me the fastest lesson I've ever learned: that **the first time a guy hits you must be the last. And if a guy does hit you, you must fight back as hard as possible, and when you get the chance, crush his nuts into nut butter.** That was what I did with Mr. SLAGIATT before saying sayonara, and I consider myself a better woman for it. As for him, I wonder if he became a better man for it, and if not, then I suspect that he at least became a better soprano.

Lesson 6 was thanks to H-BLART, "**The Hot-Blooded Artist,**" who was like a character out of a Russian novel; he was a married-but-separated visionary genius who taught me all about art, philosophy, creativity, and what happens when you subsist on a diet of fresh fruit and Ecstasy.

Yes, he was a bit "eccentric," like the time he karate-chopped a cockroach on my kitchen wall and demanded I leave it there as a "warning to all the others." And true, he was prone to delusions, like the time he hid in the windmill on the eighth hole of a mini-golf course, convinced that the Royal Canadian Mounted Police were after him. On the other hand, he was the first man who ever made me feel truly adored. On the *other* other hand, he also liked to sit in a dark closet smelling my shoes.*

H-BLART's lesson was that in small doses, **a little unpredictability and passion are fun, but in real-life doses, they're overwhelming and can sometimes lead to legal issues.** I don't know where H-BLART is today, but I think of him often, whenever I am confronted with

---

*So, I guess that would make it the other other foot.

a new idea or way of seeing the world. Or when I see a cockroach skittering across a floor.

Lesson 7 humped anything that moved. He was a complete dog. In fact, he was **The Actual Dog.**

TAD didn't look anything like I imagined he would. I'd wanted a tall, muscular dog, like a Dalmatian or a Great Dane.* TAD was a short, scrappy stray, a cross between a terrier and a sewer rat. He walked into my house and into my life and decided that I was the one for him. Me, I figured I'd give him a couple of weeks. In that time:

He chewed up two sets of eyeglasses and four pairs of shoes.

He took a crap on my friend's living room floor, in the middle of a Sunday brunch.

He bit me.

And he humped. Oh, how TAD humped.

But what TAD lacked in, well, just about everything, he made up for in personality, affection, and a Great Dane–size capacity to love. After the two-week probation period I had to admit that I'd fallen head over tail in love with him (the owner-dog kind, nothing kinky/bestial here), and he became my constant companion for the next fourteen years. When he died I wore black for a week, in honor of the tiny man in the dog suit who taught me that **it's not always love at first sight. Sometimes it's love at second, third, or fifty-seventh**

---

*That was a time when my taste in men and dogs were at par: I liked them all big, furry, playful, and not too smart.

sight; and sometimes you just gotta look past the couch-humping and give love a chance to grow.

Next up was "**The Younger Man,**" who was young enough (don't ask how young—all you need to know is that it was legal) that at first I didn't take him seriously. But he was so diligent and confident and unsullied by other women's baggage that one day, after weeks of telling him, "Hell, no," I found myself saying, "Well . . . okay!"

He was fun. He taught me how to shoot a pistol. He let me drive his fast car. He wrote me love letters—in *pen*. But I missed a couple of clues. Like the fact that my dog growled at him whenever he came over. And the fact that he was forgetful. Like he forgot to tell me when he started seeing someone else.

And that's when I remembered why I'd turned him down in the first place. I'd thought he was too young, and I was right; in the end, he was as careless with me as I'd been with other people back when I was his age. I don't blame him for doing what he did (ah, screw that—I'm holding onto this grudge like a family heirloom), but I am thankful that he got me to **Lesson 8: Trust your gut. And when your own guts fail you, trust the guts of your dog.***

And then there's **Lesson 9,** who is the culmination of all the ones who came before. He's the story that's still unfolding and the lesson that I'm still learning, and

---

*You may replace *dog* with *friends, family,* or *high-paid psychotherapist*— it's all pretty much the same thing.

he's the one who led to the kid and all the lessons I'm learning from her.*

Yes, the route was messy. And yes, it contained record numbers of bad hairstyles. But the fact is that it was only through this convoluted, partially clad scavenger hunt through humanity (and canine-ity) that I was able to find my way home. And yes, there may have been a few "additional" lessons along the way† (like "Just because a guy takes your mom to the Academy Awards, that doesn't mean that he's 'The One,'" "Beware of dudes with facial tattoos," and "Don't get engaged just because your lease is up")—those I'll save for my next book, "Laughing on the Outside, Farting on the Inside," available in bookstores never.

And maybe in preemptively sharing these stories with my daughter, by the time she's falling in and out of love/like/loathe/lust, she'll have learned that, just as everyone who enters her life becomes a part of her story, *she* is a part of someone else's story—which is why it's so important to always err on the side of kindness. And adventure. But not *too* much adventure. And occasional public nudity. (But with sunscreen.)

If nothing else, my hope is that when she's fifteen, screaming, "YOU DON'T UNDERSTAND!" and slam-

---

*The husband's probably got his own set of lessons to share with the kid, though if/when he does, I'll probably skip it due to the fact that he worked at Club Med when he was in his early twenties, and that's a TMI minefield that I'd rather avoid, thanksverymuch.

† I won't say exactly how many, just enough that if anyone asks, the kid can say that once upon a time her mom had game.

ming her door so hard that my porcelain Hummel figurines (which I don't collect yet, but I'm assuming that one day I will) fall from the doilied shelf in the guest bathroom, I can hand her this book and say "Oh yes I do. Go read Chapter 12."

thirteen

THE MARRIAGE QUOTIENT

O *ne of the most startling moments of parenthood occurred when I realized that, with the arrival of this new
human, I would be forever connected to the child's father/the
husband and that the days of fantasizing divorce over his
inability to screw the tops back onto refrigerated condiment
jars were over. Apparently, I was going to have to start taking this "marriage" thing a lot more seriously.*

✦

I find it curious that when I tell people that I've been
married for ten years, they always want to know, "Howja
meet?"

The first thing to know is that it was never in my
plans; I'd always found the idea of marriage unnerving.

Just hearing the word *fiancée* makes me want to yell, "Quit acting fancy! You're not turning French—you're just getting married!"

Growing up, most little girls I knew dreamed of walking down the aisle with Prince Charming. Me, I wanted to be a bullfighter (if I'm being honest, it was more for the flashy outfits than anything else) and dreamed of being a daring, adventurous single woman, like that spunky Mary Tyler Moore.

As a teenager I fantasized about traveling the world in my red sequined cape and jodhpurs (being it was the '80s, I probably wouldn't have stood out much), always alone, but taking on many lovers—though never using the word *lovers,* as it invokes images of bad European movies, the kind that feature far too many hairy men in Speedos.

And through my twenties and early thirties, I stayed on course, thanks to excessive confidence, more courage than common sense, and an unintentionally ludicrous series of choices in men, some of whom included the military cadet, whose idea of romance was to hack the top off a champagne bottle with a sword; the manic-depressive actor who had a bad habit of staring at his own hands; and the one-night stand who left gum in my pubic hair.

Still, it was all in the name of temporary fun, and none of it threatened permanent damage to my long-term plans, or to my hair.

Until one day a friend insisted I meet this guy who worked with her husband. She was sure we would fall madly and deeply for each other, and she wanted the matchmaking credit. We all went out for drinks at an underwhelming, overpriced steak house where the guy and I both recognized immediately that we were not a love—or even a like—match. Then at some point during the course of the evening, another friend of the husband showed up.

The new guy had a gold hoop earring and a sniper's sense of humor, and we shared an immediate and easy rapport. As I left the restaurant that night I gave him my number (in spite of the earring) and demanded that he call me. When he didn't, I was astonished. Didn't he know that I was in a brief but deliberate window of sleeping around?

Finally, after an infuriatingly long wait (four days), he called. Our first date was dinner. Our second a movie. Our third was a trip to Vegas, for the wedding of the couple who'd introduced us.

And it was in Vegas, in a dank suite at Caesars Palace, after a little wine and a little making out, that I had a vision—even though I'm usually the type to make fun of people who have those sorts of things—of him and me, and a baby. (Our own baby, that is. I am not generally prone to kidnapping fantasies.)

And just like that, I went from being a woman who would never be called wife, to being half of a couple, to vowing in front of friends and family to love and honor, forever and ever, break the glass, *l'chaim*, amen.

And the rest, as they say, is history.

Or is it? (No, I say rhetorically, it is not.)

Because marriage is like a movie where the two leads find themselves handcuffed to each other with no key and facing impossible odds to overcome. The only difference is that one version lasts two hours, while the other is much, much longer, unless you're very unlucky, slip during the bouquet toss, and fall face-first into a pointy ice sculpture.

What got them there, the "Howdja meet?" question—that's just the First Act setup. How a married couple navigates the world when they realize they're about to spend their lives joined together, like Charles Grodin and Robert DeNiro in *Midnight Run* or Elizabeth Berkley and her stripper pole in *Showgirls,* that's the real story.

Some couples toss around words like *compatibility, sacrifice, romance,* or *pharmaceuticals* when explaining how they do it. Being more analytical in my thinking, I've devised a mathematical concept to express how a marriage works. I call it "The Marriage Quotient."

It is based on a scale of "workability," where "100" might be achieving lengthy mutual orgasms while gazing into each other's eyes, "50" is the moment you're about to walk into your first couple's therapy appointment, and "5" is giving a statement to the police about why you put dehydrated cat feces in your spouse's oatmeal (I'd call that a "0," except if you're cooking for your spouse, then that should count for something).

Because the science behind the concept can be difficult to understand by anyone not living inside my skull, I shall now present a series of scenarios from my own marriage, along with their corresponding marriage quotients:

EXHIBIT A

I have just returned home after a dental appointment, only to find that the lower-left quadrant of my face is not only numb, it is completely and totally paralyzed. Initially, I find the sensation to be fun, in a novel kind of way. After spending thirty minutes staring at myself in the bathroom mirror and pretending to be Daniel Day-Lewis pretending to be a character, I head over to my computer, where I make the mistake of Googling this phenomenon, thereby learning that it's an uncommon reaction to some forms of dental anesthesia; in most cases, the paralysis is temporary, but in a few it is permanent and irreversible. As I am a card-carrying member of the Jumping to Conclusions Society, I immediately transition from being mildly entertained to experiencing a full-blown panic attack, at which point I phone my husband at work. Upon hearing me sob that I might lose the use of the left half of my mouth, he is quiet for a moment and then calmly suggests, "So, I guess this means you'll be giving blow jobs on the side."

Now then: if a major earthquake or tsunami were to occur right now, you might throw this book down, leave the place that you're sitting (screaming most likely), only to arrive at your next destination with a particular opinion of my husband, i.e., that he is uncaring and perverse, and that his statement would be grounds for divorce.

But you would be *wrong,* because you'd have missed the following point: that this is one of the bravest and most loving things my husband could have said. Because he knows that the best thing he can do when he hears panic in my voice is to give me comfort. If he were married to another person (i.e., someone normal), that might mean saying something like, "It's okay, honey. I'm sure this is just a temporary situation, but if it isn't, I will still love you, even if 25 percent of your face never moves again." But for me, the most direct route to comfort is for him to say the most wickedly inappropriate thing he can think of, even—and especially—if it is at my expense.

Marriage Quotient: 85

(Getting the hang of it? Good. Let's continue.)

EXHIBIT B

We are on the freeway in heavy traffic. He is driving. I am in the passenger seat, staring out the window, sending beams of anger and loathing directly at the right side of his face via my left shoulder. We are in the middle of a fight. I can't recall the subject, probably something important like my inability to put my shoes in the closet when I come home. I am so angry that I deduce the only logical course of action is to throw myself out of the car. I estimate that we are going fifteen miles an hour; at that speed I could easily open the door, jump out, tuck, and roll. At worst I'll suffer a sprain, maybe a concussion, both of which seem in the moment to be preferable to sitting in this car with HIM. Then traffic picks up, and my tuck-and-roll plan is foiled. I am still angry when we pull up to the pizza place.

Here is where you may conclude that this story expresses a low MQ, perhaps around 40, and that our relationship is doomed because invariably, one day we will find ourselves in a traffic jam that does not let up, I will succeed at throwing myself from the car, and the husband will find himself on trial for manslaughter because of my inability to accurately gauge traffic speed.

Again, you'd be wrong. Because that is not where this story ends. It continues.

Now we are waiting at the bar of the pizza restaurant, aggressively not speaking to each other. From out of nowhere, a gentleman stumbles toward us; it's clear that he is tipsy. He sways back and forth while making polite small talk and then turns to the husband and poses the question, "Do you like your wife's stinky drawers?" The eyes of the husband go wide, at which point he clears his throat and mumbles something like, "Begyourpardon?"

The man delivers a stirring monologue, in the middle of this family restaurant, about how deeply he loves his wife and how much he appreciates and reveres her "stinky drawers." And while he rhapsodizes, he reaches into his pocket and pulls out a cotton handkerchief to wipe his brow; only after he mops and refolds does it become clear that the handkerchief is not a handkerchief but is, in fact, a pair of his wife's aforementioned stinky drawers.

Without a word, the husband smiles and grabs my hand. I take his gesture both as a signal to me that (a) should this social interaction get any weirder, he will protect me; also (b) to indicate that if he must experience this stranger-than-fiction moment, he is glad to be sharing it with me.

The man bids us adieu, then stumbles out of the restaurant and into a cab, headed for, I'm guessing, his home and his probably pantyless wife. Moments after that the husband and I are sitting in a booth, eating pizza, laughing, and thanking the universe for providing us with moments like this. And when we return home that night, I put my shoes away.

Marriage Quotient: 74

EXHIBIT C

The husband has encouraged me to take a night off with friends while he stays home and takes care of our daughter, who is about a year old at this point.

I am driving with my friend Renee. When my cell phone rings, I ask Renee to answer the call; she does. It's the husband. She puts him on speakerphone.

"Hi!" I say.

"Hey . . . " His voice is strained, his breath shallow. I recognize this "hey"; something bad has happened.

"Is everything all right?"

"I—I have to ask you something . . . "

I pull over to the side of the road. "What's wrong? Is the baby okay?"

"Did you . . . Have you . . ." His voice through the speaker is quiet and strained. "Were you sewing today?"

"Was I . . . *sewing*?" I ask, just to make sure I've heard him right.

"Were you sewing?" he asks again.

"No. Why?"

"Are you sure?" His voice becomes louder, more insistent. "You're *sure* you weren't recently sewing?"

I look to Renee in the passenger seat. She is as confused and disturbed by this line of questioning as I am.

"What happened?" I ask. "Did you step on a needle or something?"

"It's—it's bad. Are you sure you weren't sewing?

"Why do you keep asking me that? Oh, God, is the baby hurt? Did she eat a pin?! Will you please tell me what's happened?"

He takes a breath. "I just went to the bathroom. I think—I . . . I passed a huge tapeworm. Oh, my God, I'm never eating sushi again . . . "

I pause to think for a moment. "Oh, wait. I did floss my teeth this morning . . . "

Silence. Then, the sound of a toilet lid opening.

"Oh. Yeah. That was it."

We hang up the phone, and Renee and I continue on our way to TGI Fridays.

This example displays deep strength at the core of our marriage. In the first place, the husband showed care and concern when he encouraged me to spend the evening with a friend; he also demonstrated his trust in me when he bravely shared his fears and concerns with me. I, in turn, showed deep abiding respect and restraint by waiting until we had hung up the phone to laugh with my friend in silent stereo until our faces were soaked and our diaphragm muscles were destroyed.

Marriage Quotient: 83 (plus 10 bonus points for letting me tell this story) = 93

EXHIBIT D

I am standing in the shower, enjoying the peaceful sensation of warm water cascading down my body when, unbeknownst to me, the husband strolls into the bathroom unannounced and unleashes a sneeze that is so loud and violent—and, dare I say, hostile—it's as though a bullet has been fired directly into my ear: it's an atomic bomb of sound and snot that startles me so badly it gives me whiplash . . . naked whiplash. My immediate reaction is to bellow a loud and angry, "WHAT THE FUUUUUUHHH—!!!" Then I stop, compose myself, and utter a polite "Gesundheit," to which he responds with a quiet, "Thank you."

You may conclude that this moment demonstrates my ability to transcend petty feelings and momentary frustration. I would respectfully disagree and submit that if he loved me more, he'd figure out some way, perhaps through surgical means, to never, ever sneeze again. Clearly, this is an area that needs to be worked on. By him.

Marriage quotient: 17

~

I could go on, but I think you get my points:

1. that what happens in Vegas does not stay in Vegas, but leads to a Jewish wedding
2. that my social theory and math skills are questionable at best
3. that partial facial paralysis, within the bonds of matrimony, can in some cases be considered a turn-on

And if you take only one thing away, let it be this: that marriage works because of its power to act as a buffer against the human trials of fear, anger, sadness, and some strange man's wife's underwear.

fourteen

THE BINKY WAR DIARIES

DECEMBER 28, 2006, 11:26 P.M.

O ur daughter is a few hours old and emitting a sound that could shatter a pair of glass eyes. She has been crying since the moment she flew out of me, and neither my husband nor I have the foggiest idea how to stop it.

The husband looks like a character in a psychological thriller who has just discovered that everything in his life is a lie, while I—a person who has just been torn apart from the inside out by a thrashing, indignant nine-pound garden slug—can't be trusted to have a useful thought about anything right now.

Suddenly, there is a wizened old nurse in the room, though neither of us saw her enter. She leans over the baby and sticks a complimentary green pacifier into the baby's yell-hole. The baby closes her gaping maw around it, begins to suckle, and then is quiet, for the first time in her life.

The H and I are struck mute with gratitude. The thousand-year-old nurse says, "You're lucky. Not all babies take to it. That Binky will bring you a lot of peace in the days ahead." And as the ancient woman slips out of the room, that is exactly how we feel: lucky.

FEBRUARY 23, 2007

They call the first three months of a baby's life "the fourth trimester." I call it the apocalypse. There is so much sleeplessness and tears and vomit and random bodily fluids projecting themselves skyward—it's the third circle of hell, and it smells like the inside of a Lollapalooza porta-potty.

And the Binky, the Binky has turned into a tool of the chaos. Sure, it stops the screaming, but only when it's firmly embedded in the child's scream-cave, which is almost never, because this demanding beast hasn't figured out how to use her G.D. hands yet. Her tendency to fumble and drop the pacifier is endless, and unless one of us dives from forty feet across the room to retrieve and stick it back in her mouth within .05 nanoseconds, she unleashes a 90-decibel warning that sounds like a backward Latin curse from the Book of the Dead.

Look, I understand that it's "illegal" to duct tape a pacifier to a baby's face. Fine. But we can't even glue it to her hand? Since when are we living in a fascist state?!

JUNE 12, 2007

We are hostages in our own home. We cannot leave the house without having a minimum of three pacifiers within arm's reach at all times. Last week we were stuck in freeway traffic when I realized that, although there are upwards of forty-two Binkies littering the floor of our living room (not counting the seven lint-crusted ones under the couch), there was not one to be found in the car, where we were.

For two solid hours.

Of screaming.

Worse, now that she's teething, she's begun grinding Binky back and forth in her porcelain nubs so that it makes a low, ominous *SCREEEEEEE SCREEEEEEE SCREEEEEEE* sound, like something out of a Japanese horror film.

A friend suggested cutting a pinhole in Binky to "make it less satisfying for her," so I spent last night sticking safety pins through every one of her Binkies. It made me feel desperate and dirty, like some girl popping holes in condoms on prom night. When I sneaked the compromised pacifiers back into her rotation, the child didn't seem to care—she went on happily sucking on Binky. The only difference is that it now whistles in a high-pitched tone that causes my ears to bleed.

I know I should be thankful for something that gives my child comfort and joy, but I'm not. The H thinks I'm resentful because of all the breast-feeding problems the pacifier caused.* He put it this way: "It's like when a dude gets cock-blocked by another guy. You got tit-blocked by a Binky."

So yeah, Diary, you could say that I'm just a tad resentful.

MARCH 6, 2008

Spent the day Googling *speech impediments* and *orthodontic expenses* and staring into the kid's open mouth while she napped. I am now positive that Binky is morphing her little smile into a *Deliverance*-style maze of buckteeth and racism.

Being that the husband is out of town for the weekend, I decide to take action. (I'll admit that my record in situations like these is not so great. Last time he left town, I got an asymmetrical haircut; the time before that, I signed up for the "Beef of the Month Club" from a guy driving through the neighborhood in a '79 custom van. But this urge takes hold of me, and I am powerless to ignore it.)

I let the kid watch eleven back-to-back episodes of *Caillou* while I rounded up all of the pacifiers in the house and hid them in a bag in the garage. Then guilt and paranoia kicked in, so I pumped her up with candy and chased her around the house, tickling her until she passed out from sheer exhaustion.

As I laid her down in her crib, I silently congratulated myself for taking Binky by the balls. This is going

---

*As painfully detailed in Chapter 3, "Spoiled Milk."

to work, because parenting is instinctual—in a way that buying beef products is not.

MARCH 7, 2008, 3:00 A.M.

I awoke when I heard a noise in the middle of the night, but when I got up to investigate I saw that it was just the dog humping my slipper. I tiptoed past the kid's room, where I could hear her breathing deeply, sleeping soundly, making it through her first night without Binky.

That passy's ass is *grass*.

The husband will be pleased with my success. He will also be annoyed by it. It will be a total win-win for me.

MARCH 7, 2008, 6:30 A.M.

The kid is still sleeping so soundly that I have time to shower and make her pancakes for breakfast. Cheers to the power of intuition . . . and to the effectiveness of cold turkey, well done!

MARCH 7, 2008, 7:00 A.M.

I sneaked into her room and leaned in to lay a kiss on the back of her head. As she rolled over sleepily, what did I see hanging out of her face but A GODDAMN BINKY!!!!!

WHAT IN THE FRIGGIN FRIG—?! I was SURE I'd gotten them all . . . Maybe it was stuck under the mattress . . . or between the crib and the wall . . . or maybe Lucifer himself appeared in a puff of sulfur and stuck one in her face to pay me back for that time when I was twelve and swore on a Bible that I was related to Kristy McNichol . . .

I just reread what I wrote, and all I can think is that I must be losing my mind.

I'm off now to the garage to retrieve the hidden pacifiers.

Seems Binky has won the battle.

But the war is still far from over.

FEBRUARY 2009

BINKY STILL OWNS US.

AUGUST 22, 2009

In light of recent developments, I have decided that my only course of action is to support my child in her pacifier habit.

To that end, in an attempt to fully understand her "addiction," last night after she went to sleep I set a timer for five minutes, inserted one of the Binkies into my mouth, and, as God is my witness, *I sucked*.

What follows is a rough transcript of my thoughts during that time:

Breathe . . . suck . . .

Breathe . . . suck . . .

What the shitting shit am I doing? What if the government is recording me through the baby monitor, and this ends up going viral on Facebook or Twitter or some other site I'm too unhip to know about?! Though this is far from the dumbest thing I have ever done, it will ruin me!

Get a hold of yourself, Stein . . . You're doing this for your child. Any loving, neurotic parent would do the same. Stay with this.

Breathe . . . suck . . .

Breathe . . . suck . . .

Wow. I suck loudly.

Okay . . . Now I've got a good groove going.

Breathe . . . suck . . .

This actually feels sort of nice.

Mmmmkay. Just gonna let my mind wander . . .

Breathe . . . suck . . . breathe . . . suck . . .

Wow, this takes me back to my college days . . . Except this thing would've been lit and I'd have been laughing hysterically at a piece of cheddar cheese.

Breathe . . . suck . . .

It feels so tiny in my mouth. Huh. I wonder how my ex-boyfriend Doug is doing?

Breathe . . . suck . . .

I feel really . . . good. And . . . satisfied. Just sucking and "being" like this, I feel so powerful, as though I could do anything . . . Like join the Peace Corps! Or move to Ghana! Or help birth a two-headed wildebeest!

I could really get used to this. I wonder if they make these in chocolate flav—

And there goes the alarm.

The baby crack experiment is over.

It was definitely an interesting, illuminating, and not altogether unpleasant experience. In the long run, however, I don't think it's for me; on the other hand, neither is macramé, and I didn't kick my grandma to the curb over that.

So the kid likes to suck on a plastic teat. Who cares? We all have our guilty pleasures. As a child I used to pick up chewed gum from the sidewalk and eat it. Didn't hurt me in the long run; if anything, it probably strengthened my immune system, and most certainly helped me to become a thrifty consumer. Back in elementary school, (*Name Redacted*) was a well-known booger eater but then grew up to become a respected member of Canadian Parliament—so really, who are we to judge?

NOVEMBER 11, 2010

During a walk today an old lady smiled at us, "My, my, isn't she a little bit old for a passy?" I wanted to respond, "As a matter of fact, you righteous old gasbag, yes she is!" But I didn't. And when an under-three-year-old at the park yelled at my now almost-four-year-old sucking on her pacifier, "WHY YOU SUCK ON DAT? DON'T DO DAT!" I suppressed my desire to walk right up to him and slap his mother.

I can deal with my own judgment—but now the ass-faces of the world are weighing in.

So I did what I always do when wrestling with a deeply troubling parenting concern: I turned to the opinions of perfect strangers and faceless trolls. This time, however, the Internet was most helpful, and I learned about "The Binky Fairy," a recent Tooth Fairy–adjacent addition to popular kid bamboozlery.

As per the "mythology," I tell the child all about the magical creature who comes in the night to take Binkies from big kids so that she can give them to poor, unfortunate babies without Binkies—and in their place leaves unimagined treasures.

The child was intrigued. "HOW WILL I KNOW WHEN SHE'S COMING?" she asked. I offered to text the Binky Fairy and check on her availability.

"Looks like she has an opening tonight . . ."

Surprisingly, the kid said she was ready.

We're going for it. Tonight!

7:30 P.M.

We put the Binkies in a special box and left it on her dresser. She said she's happy for the baby who will get her Binky, then asked how big and strong the Binky Fairy is, and will she be using a sleigh to bring all those treasures?

I just turned out the light. Shouldn't be long now.

8:47 P.M.

Was surprised to find her awake, but just barely. Her eyes were drooping. NOW, it shouldn't be long, now.

10:06 P.M.

MAYDAY! MAYDAY! THE WHEELS ARE OFF THE WAGON! The kid is jumping up and down on her bed, wild-eyed; she's wired and babbling aggressively. She's not upset—but it seems she has forgotten how to sleep. Is this what happens when a heroin addict goes through withdrawal?

10:25 P.M.

I rubbed her back until my hands were chafed. She finally passed out face-first into her pillow.

SHIT! Just realized I have no Binky Fairy booty to seal the deal.

Just yelled to the husband, "HOLD DOWN THE FORT!"—am off to the late-night Target that's open 'til 11:00. Wish me luck!

10:52 P.M.

TARGET

NOT-SO-GREAT AREA OF TOWN

I grab a cart, careening through the aisles toward the toy section . . . double back to grab some toilet paper and a jar of Nutella (on special) . . . then on to the aisles filled with pink, where I shop like one of those contestants on a daytime game show, grabbing whatever I can get my hands on. A pink bedazzled pillow. A Barbie book. A hula hoop. And the first sparkly greeting card I see, one that says "CONGRATULATIONS TO A FINE BOY ON HIS BAR MITZVAH," because who gives a snot, she can't read yet.

I check out, the last customer in the store, and speed home, praying to God that I don't get carjacked by gangbangers who will kill me when all I have to offer is a carload of pink crap and an overdrawn ATM card.

Once home I compose a "letter" from the Binky Fairy. In it I go into great detail about the intended Binky recipient—she's got a real sob story: she's got no Binky, no toys. I even drop hints that she's legally blind. If my kid isn't moved by this, then she's not human.

7:00 A.M.

Was awakened by the kid screaming.

"SHE CAME! THE BINKY FAIRY CAME!"

She was ecstatic about the gifts left in her room and listened patiently as I read aloud the letter from the Binky Fairy, stuttering and stumbling as I did in order to maintain the illusion that I've never seen it before (I am nothing if not a committed liar).

MONDAY, NOVEMBER 14, 2010

The weekend was a little rough—there were a few tears and some "WHY DID B HAVE TO GO?'s," but the child seems to have accepted her new normal. Also, turns out she's pretty good with the hula hoop.

As we dropped the kid off at preschool we watched as she told her friends all about her visit from the Binky Fairy. Rebecca—a loud-talking redhead with a tough-sounding lisp—listened with interest. Then Rebecca asked point-blank, "WHY DON'T YOU JUTH THUCK YOUR THUMB?" and demonstrated, shoving her paint-covered thumb into her mouth.

And just like that, our former pacifier addict, the altruistic Binky donor, became one of the most committed thumb suckers the world has ever known.

fifteen

THE MOST WONDERFUL TIME
OF THE YEAR

The month before she turned three, my daughter asked me the question that I had been fearing ever since she was a glimmer in my fallopian tube: "What's Christmas?" she asked. When I opened my mouth to answer, all that came out was a raspy, choking sound. It was more awkward than the time she saw me coming out of the shower and asked me why I was wearing socks on my "kiki."*

Here's the thing: as we've established, I was born to a pair of dope-smoking, radical hippie Jewish intellectuals

---

*I'm guessing I don't need to explain what "kiki" means, but suffice it to say I have not had it waxed in a long time. I.e.: Ever.

in Winnipeg, Canada. As has not been established, I didn't know a lot of Jews in Winnipeg, Canada, and I knew even fewer dope-smoking, radical hippie intellectual ones.[*]

My parents were "free thinkers" (when they weren't stoned, anyway) and felt that organized religion was a "thin construct of a shallow, emotionally enfeebled culture." As a kid I didn't have the foggiest idea what that meant (I still don't), but it didn't matter because on Sunday mornings while my friends were waking up at seven, pulling on itchy wool dresses and dusty tights for church, I was cocooned in a warm blankie, laughing at *Bugs Bunny* cartoons while jamming spoonfuls of Count Chocula into my yap. There I was, all those Sunday mornings, gloating at my good fortune with brown marshmallows stuck in my teeth.

And then December would roll around.

Hanukkah would slide past our house without a nod, but I was fine with that. Since I didn't know any other Jews—for a while I considered them mythical creatures—as far as I was concerned, Hanukkah was the weird, distant, creepy mouth breather of an uncle that you don't want to spend one night with, never mind eight.

No, my soul-scarring pain belonged to Christmas. My holy grail day, the one holiday I desired more than anything in the world. The songs! The gingerbread! And the trees. All those adolescent pines garishly adorned with tinsel, lights, and big shiny balls, so wrong yet so right, as tasteless

---

[*]Let the record show that I have since learned that Winnipeg is a veritable hotbed of Canadian Jewry. Clearly I should have gotten out more.

and tawdry as a ten-year-old Brooke Shields in high heels and hooker makeup. Oh, Christmas Tree indeed!

But in the Stein household, Christmas was the most despicable of religious holidays. My parents rejected its rampant, crass commercialization, its Judeo-Christian-fascist hypocrisy (their indecipherable phrasing, not mine), though I think they mostly just resented having to spend time with extended family who didn't approve of their "alternative lifestyle" (i.e., their frequent consumption of pot brownies).

But my parents, God (or whoever) bless 'em, had the presence of mind to recognize that, even though they had their principles, our family was weird enough already. Depriving their kids of presents during the holiday season, well, that was just one toke over the line.

And lo, "Stein Day" came to be.

"Stein Day" fell on December 26 (Boxing Day, a.k.a., "The Great Canadian Fire Sale"), when sometime around midafternoon, Mom, Dad, and the big blue Rambler station wagon would pull into the garage, loaded down with half-price Legos, out-of-the-box Erector Sets, and several bags of Chinese food. And while the kids happily played with their loot, Mom and Dad would spoon out the chop suey and smoke a joint or two or seven, and that was that. Happy Stein Day, everybody! No gate-crashing relatives stinking up the bathroom, no toasts about gross things like family togetherness, no commie-fascist-Hallmark bullshit. Just fun!

By the time I was old enough to appreciate it, Stein Day had evolved into something even more casual, if that's possible (and yes, it was). My teenage brothers couldn't be paid to hang out with their parents, even if they did have the best pot in town. And the magical, cavernous Rambler, now deceased, had been replaced by a VW Bug in which my mom would drive me to Kmart, where she would hand me twenty bucks with the instructions to "get yourself something and bring me back the change."

While I truly appreciated the strings-free cash, I wanted *more*. More what, I didn't quite know. Just more **something.**

The year I turned eleven I asked my mom if we could take a crack at this whole Christmas thing, maybe get a small tree? She laughed long and hard and then gave me her stock answer of "Don't be ridiculous," because underneath all that tie-dye beat the heart of a pragmatic dictator.

That was the moment that my personal search for Yuletide satisfaction began.

On Christmas morning, before anyone in my house was awake, I'd shower, get dressed in my fanciest duds and snow boots, then leave the house to make my rounds. I'd have breakfast with the Taylors, brunch with the Herberts, and dinner with the Ricketts.

After gorging myself at each stop, I'd do a little reconnaissance, using the opportunity to test-drive all that freshly unwrapped Christmas booty (even though I'd deemed "Stein Day" lacking, all spiritual dissatisfaction aside I did have twenty dollars of toys to pick out). It's how I learned that Sea Monkeys suffer from a horrible case of false advertising and that an Easy-Bake Oven, even if it is just a lightbulb encased in plastic, is pretty damned spectacular.

An unexpected (but welcome) side effect of my Christmas Day Drop-In tactic was that I'd invariably cash in on the sympathies of my friends' parents, who were completely confused and horrified by the notion of "Stein Day," which meant I'd usually get sent home with at least one floater gift from under each tree. (As a result, to this day, I have enough address books, photo albums, and Santa-shaped candles to last me the rest of my life.)

And then I'd walk home with a bellyful of Christmas goose and fruitcake and armfuls of gifts and leftover mincemeat pie, but with an odd feeling, like I'd cheated the system but still didn't win.

Then when I turned fifteen, something remarkable happened—well, remarkable for a fifteen-year-old. I fell madly in something-like-love with a boy who wooed me by reading to me from his hip youth Bible, *The Way* (which featured colored photos of Jesus, who, it turns out, was a stone-cold fox). On our first Christmas Eve together, he took me to his church. It was a small, homey Presbyterian joint, and as we held hands and sang songs about frankincense and reindeer, I felt a deep sense of warmth and belonging. The feeling remained, even after we left the church, and I felt it later that night while he was feeling me up in the backseat of his Pontiac, my heart overflowing with hormones, emotion, and the true spirit of Christmas.

Unfortunately, my swollen heart was mutilated about a week later when he broke it off, saying that he didn't have enough love in his heart for both Jesus and me. Just like that, my own private Christmas was ruined. That year, the year that Jesus stole my boyfriend (then subsequently gave him to Tanya Bendarchuk), was the year I made peace with the fact that I would never make peace with Christmas.

And I didn't. As I exited puberty and entered adulthood, every year became an experimental improvisation of holiday revelry; one year I'd put up a tree and decorate it ironically with sneakers and fake mustaches; the next year I'd ignore it entirely. Sure, I'd enjoy a slice of Christmas ham when offered, and who was I to say no to a mug of five-thousand-calorie eggnog? But the older I got, the more estranged we became. Christmas was like a Facebook friend that I'd stalk now and then, but I wouldn't dream of inviting him to crash at my house for a week.

By the time the husband showed up, I was long past my Christmas obsession.

Enter, the kid.

The husband and I agreed that we should probably mark the holiday season in some way, because, like my parents, we're weird enough already. I had a feeling it would end up looking a lot like Stein Day;* maybe we'd throw a few chocolate dreidels into the mix, but beyond that I figured we'd be loading up the Rambler and gorging ourselves on lo mein.

And that's exactly what we did.

For exactly one year.

---

*Except without the bong.

Because (if you're like us) one day you discover that children are humans with opinions and questions of their own, and that your lazy nonsolution is not a solution at all.

And while I did come to appreciate "Stein Day" (and not just for its cocktail-party conversation appeal), it didn't fit my new family: For one, marijuana makes me paranoid 82 percent of the time. And second, half of the people in my marriage were bar mitzvahed when they were thirteen. Add in the fact that the husband (a.k.a. the bar-mitzvah boy) began to feel what I now understand is a common experience of new parents—the pull of his religious roots. And so we found a sweet little Jewish preschool, a block from Chicago's Wrigley Field. A place where the kid could learn about Jewish holidays, tradition, and identity in an open, welcoming environment, and we could snack on the occasional loaf of challah as we strolled home through the throngs of drunk and disorderly Cubs fans.

We had chosen our team (Judaism/Cubbies); we had a direction; we were finally on a path.

So when the almost-four-year-old child asked, "WHY CAN'T WE GET A CHRISTMAS TREE?"—our united-front answer, "Because we're Jewish," was the end of the conversation. Or at least it should have been.

꩜

Cut to: a Tuesday afternoon in mid-December. I was spending a delightful afternoon shopping for HVAC filters at the local Home Depot when I became lost among the forty acres of Christmas-decoration displays and stopped in my tracks at the sight of a sparkly bush/tree/plant in a pot no taller than me.

It was spindly, prickly, and shapeless. This wasn't a Christmas Tree; it wasn't a Hanukkah Bush. It was a glorious HOLIDAY SHRUB, and though I can't quite explain what came over me, in that moment I realized that it was the answer to all of our/my prayers.

Ten minutes later I found myself forty dollars poorer, but one Holiday-Shrub-jammed-into-the-back-of-our-SUV richer. I headed out of the parking lot and then called the husband to give him the great news!

He didn't see it as great news. He was actually kinda annoyed that I'd made an executive decision on a subject over which we would need at least a week of arguing and obsessing.

Passive-aggressive expert that I am, my immediate impulse was just to override his concerns, present my daughter with her wonderful new Holiday Shrub, and henceforth be the titleholder of the Best Parent Award. But my cooler brain cell prevailed; this was going to take a little time and a lot of finesse. And if not that, then some harsh words followed by several well-focused silent treatments.

But in that moment, with just twenty minutes before I had to pick up the kid from her preschool, I pulled a quick detour by the home of my friend Christina, whose name is no coincidence: her holiday rituals are staggering—she spends more in a month on tinsel than I do in a year on my hair.

I carried the HS up to Christina's second-floor apartment (stabbing myself in the face with its hypodermic-like needles as I went), set it on the landing, and rang the bell. I figured I could leave it with her for a day or two, or as long as it took for me to talk the husband into letting it live with us.

As I made my way down the stairwell, Christina peeked her head out of her door.

"MERRY CHRISTMAS!" I called out.

"GET THAT UGLY-ASS CACTUS OUT OF MY HALLWAY" she called back.

I explained my predicament—that I was on my way to pick up the kid and couldn't risk her seeing the HS before clearing it with the husband. Christina's thoughtful response was that I should "GET IT THE HELL OUT OF HERE RIGHT NOW."

I dragged the HS down the stairs (more facial stabbing), shoved it into the back of my truck, and, with just seconds to spare, sped to the preschool, where I found the kid proudly spinning the clay dreidel she'd made that afternoon. It looked like a four-sided blob of sparkly fecal matter, but as we walked to the car the kid babbled excitedly about the upcoming "Festival of Lights," and as I buckled the kid into her car seat, I found myself getting choked up at her enthusiasm for this relatively minor Jewish holiday.

"SOMETHING SMELLS LIKE GUM!" she said, unaware that twelve inches behind her head, doused in fake pine scent, was the answer to her dreams. Or were they mine? I was no longer sure.

When we arrived home, the husband hugged me. "I've thought it over . . . Let's do it," he said. "Let's keep the tree."

"No," I whispered. "I'm taking it back tomorrow. No tree for us. We're Jews. Big Jews. Jew Jew Jew Jew Jews."

The husband rolled his eyes and threw his hands up in a particular combination of exasperation and acceptance that I have come to know so well.

Driving the child the next morning to preschool—her adorably Jew-y preschool—I felt at peace. It had taken years of inner struggle, but I was finally, truly ready to put my Christmas obsession into permanent storage. I was so focused on my admirable decision-making skills, in fact, that I hadn't noticed the flashing blue and red lights behind me. It wasn't until I heard the siren that I pulled over, in front of the kid's preschool.

The officer stomped toward my window.

"You know you were goin' twenty-five in a fifteen-mile-an-hour school zone?"

"Was I? I didn't realize. We didn't want to be late. My daughter actually goes to preschool here . . . "

"Oh yeah?" The officer seemed to soften. "My niece goes there too. It's a sweet place." He flashed a kind smile to my daughter, who smiled back.

Then his expression turned to puzzlement as he looked beyond the kid to the green needle-y branches behind her head. He then shook his head and turned back to me, his face betrayed by the weariness of someone who gets lied to on a regular basis.

"Nice 'Christmas Tree' you got there."

Before I could explain myself, and just as the words "HOLIDAY SHRUB . . . " tried to flee from my lips, I heard an ear-splitting squeal, and in the rearview I watched as my kid's head rotated 180 degrees.

"MOMMA, YOU GOT ME A CHRISTMAS TREE?! YAYYYYYY!!!!"

There were so many things I could have/should have said. Instead, I just kept my mouth shut and held out my hand as Officer Greenberg handed me my ticket.

⌀

That night we stood, the husband, the kid, and I: three Jews hanging Christmas lights and blobby Hanukkah decorations around a sharp, slouching bush, praying to God (or somebody) that nobody would put an eye out.

"DO YOU THINK SANTA WILL COME?" the kid asked.

I looked at the husband. He shrugged.

"Sure," I sighed. "Why not?"

And he did. And it was good. And it was all thanks to a cranky police officer who'd forced our hands into making a simple, deliberate decision—that we would create our own holiday rituals, starting with the concepts of Inclusion and Joy. So this year there will be a tree and a menorah, stockings and dreidels, bagels and turkey, and a nighttime visit from some milk-and-cookie-fueled chubster in a red getup. And the following day we'll invite our friends over for a Stein Day dinner. There will be plenty of gratitude for flexible family, and the halls will ring with singing and the voices of well-wishers calling out: *"Merry Christmukkah-SteinMas to All, and to All a Good Night!"*

sixteen

THE VERY BAD HAIR DAY

It's the smell that hits you first. Like a mixture of Kool-Aid, nail-polish remover, and dirty nickels soaked in spit.

As we enter, the four-year-old child emits a squeal that causes my pupils to dilate. I can't exactly blame her; this place—a hair-salon entry into the lucrative children's market—has been scientifically engineered for the delight of her species.

We are greeted at reception by a disturbingly cheerful, tiara-wearing, Tigger tattoo–having girl named Caitlin, whose every sentence! Is punctuated by! An Exclamation!! Mark!!!!! She ushers us through the salon, giving us the apparently earth-shattering news that "YOU'RE WITH JENNA! OH EM GEE, I LOOOVE JENNA!"

141

The place feels vaguely like a Chuck E. Cheese, only more hygienic and 15 percent less barfy. Colored lights flash on cartoon murals of oily-looking princes and brainless princesses; happy clients suck on lollipops in barber chairs built to look like race cars, rocket ships, and royal carriages; while pop music by singers with dolphin-pitched voices fills the air.

It's every kid's dream—and for me a nightmare of *Saw 14* proportions.

I clench my jaw, personally offended that this place has the audacity to exist. I know I sound like my future grandma self when I say this, but What The Hell Have We Become? When I was a kid my mom would grab her pinking shears,* tell me to shut my eyes, and eight minutes of dangerous-implement wielding later, I had a perfectly good haircut that, if I tilted my head to one side, was pretty much passable.

And if I sound crotchety right now, that's because crotchety is the condition in which I find myself as I take in this overstimulating, acid-trip panorama through my strained and baggy red-rimmed eyes.

The fact is that three weeks ago, said child did extract from me, in a weak moment,† a promise that I would bring her to this place for a haircut. And even though said child cannot seem to remember that "Tues-

---

*Those weird jagged sewing scissors that are great if you want to create a reasonable facsimile of your cousin Vern's teeth; other than that, they're totally useless.

†A moment that may or may not have involved me saying, "Yes, whatever you want, just please leave Mommy alone right now so she can finish crying to *The Notebook*."

day" does not follow "November" on the calendar, she was able to recall that "TODAY IS HAIRCUT DAY!"—about ten minutes before the appointment. And though I may be a crank of immense proportions, I will not renege on our deal because I am a woman of honor. (Also, they made me give them a credit card number to hold the reservation, and there's a twenty-five-dollar fee to cancel. Jerks.)

My daughter eeny-meeny-minies between a hot-air-balloon chair and a royal-carriage chair (she "wins" the hot-air balloon, then picks the carriage anyway—clearly her sense of honor is not as strong as mine) and is then greeted by Jenna, yet another horrifyingly bright-eyed and cartoon-character-tattooed maiden who will be cutting the kid's hair at a cost of approximately a dollar per strand.

After a quick conference with Jenna about what we're looking for: price (low) and style (who cares), I warn the child that she is not to request any extras (no bows, tiaras, gowns, or live Clydesdales) and to not even *think* about playing the extortionist Claw Grabber Game in the corner, and then I slither over to the bench to stew in what is probably number 3 in my list of Top-Ten Nonspecific Yet Supremely Foul Moods I Have Been In.

I take a seat in the waiting area, where my thighs—the ones that have been struggling to escape the ill-fitting jean skort I'd thrown on before running out the door—are sticking to the painted wooden bench under them, making a nauseating *FWAP FWAP* sound every time I move, while twelve inches from my head an unattended toddler pounds away at the paddles on a retro Strawberry Shortcake pinball machine (*BLAPATTA-BLAPATTA-BLAPATTA*).

Shifting uncomfortably (*FWAP FWAP*), I mull over the seventeen-item to-do list (CHANGE OIL, POST OFFICE, VET BILL) that is weighing heavily on my mind (PAY TRAFFIC TICKET, PICK UP PRESCRIPTION), or rather on my hand, where I wrote it (*BLAPPATA BLAPPATA BLAPPATA*) in pen while driving here because I couldn't get it together (*FWAP FWAP FWAP*) to buy a friggin notepad (BUY FRIGGIN NOTEPAD).

I glance out the window and lock eyes with a sullen, mean-faced lady wearing a hat that appears to have been knitted from a knotted-up bundle of yak hair. Then I realize that the window is actually a mirror, and the mean-faced lady is me. And PS: it's not a hat.

I reach up and attempt to rearrange the yarn ball, but it's pointless. I close my eyes and make a mental note to add "HAVE HAIR BALL REMOVED FROM HEAD" to my ever-growing to-do list, because of course I can't find a pen to add to my list of hand-inked chores.

A rhinestone-encrusted head rises up from behind the faux-castle reception desk.

"EFF WHY EYE! YOU KNOW WE DO BIG GIRLS TOO, RIGHT???"

Let me get this straight, crown-wearing commoner, I think. You really believe that I'm going to hop up into one of those thrones and submit to having my hair cut by some chirpy-faced, perky-chested beauty-school dropout with Disney characters tattooed on her arms? If I had an ounce of energy right now, I would fly at you like Uma Thurman in *Kill Bill* and pluck out your left—

"IT'S 'MOM-DAY MON-DAY,' AND MOM'S ARE FREEEEE!!!!!"

—then again, perhaps I thought-spoke too soon.

"I THINK MILLIE'S AVAILABLE! SHE'S OUR MOST REQUESTED!"

Caitlin picks up a phone and then squeals into it with a level of excitement I've only ever seen on *The Price Is Right*, "I HAVE A WALK-IN!"

After a moment she hangs up. "YOU'RE GOING TO ADORE MILLIE!"

Don't tell me what to adore, I want to say. You don't know me, and if you did, you'd stop talking in that particular way that makes my spine want to shoot out of my back. But of course, I don't actually say any of that out loud. I'm far too annoyed/Canadian/passive-aggressive to do that. But the fact is that I do need a haircut, and it's not like I have a regular stylist that I'd be cheating on.* Also, in some perverse way I'm looking forward to the opportunity of spreading my bad mood like a lip herpes.

---

*I've never been able to make that kind of commitment because I can't handle the small talk required of the stylist-stylee relationship; I worry that, due to my captive status, I will blurt out something inappropriate, and my discomfort gets magnified in the presence of all those scissors and hot styling implements, so I just stay quiet, which then causes me to worry that I'm offending the stylist, who I'm certain is quietly resenting me as she or he works, taking it out on my hair in ways that I won't see until the next time I wash it. It's exhausting, but rather than confront my feelings around this particular neurosis, I've just found it easier to go someplace new whenever I need a haircut. It's my "Cut and Run" policy.

A velvet doorway curtain swishes, and through it walks Millie. Not exactly as I'd pictured her, Millie's about thirty—make that forty—years older than I'd imagined. And bigger. About the size of two Caitlins and a Jenna. No Tigger tattoos on her fleshy arms, but there is bounce aplenty. And her chest is not so much perky as it is microwave-size, and restrained by what I'm guessing must be a very powerful, military-issue brassiere.

Millie beckons for me to follow her. I do, drafting behind her wide backside and taking in her peculiar smell—part sweet, part salty, part dill. Not bad, exactly, though it does make me the tiniest bit hungry.

She guides me past the race-car chair that, had I been in a better mood, I might have rallied for, and into a plain old stylist chair that's a little more my size and speed.

Millie covers me in a pink smock that's been painted to look like a princess gown. She has difficulty with the tie in the back and mumbles something behind my head—"Boolsheet cack"—which I realize are the first words I've heard come out of her mouth, and which, if you say them quietly to yourself (as I did, several times), you come to realize is some pretty powerful profanity, filtered through her vaguely eastern European accent.

I look around the room to see if anyone has heard her. No, seems all the other stylists are occupied with their hyperactive, sugar-bombed clients.

Millie wets my hair down with a spray bottle filled with a solution that smells like straight bubblegum water and begins combing out the nest on my head. "How old?"

She juts her chin in the direction of my child, who at this moment is across the room, beaming as Jenna tosses into her hair a handful of sparkles that I will be vacuuming out of our carpets for the next eighteen months.

"She's four years old."

Millie emits a series of staccato grunts. "*Mmh mmh mmh*," she says, nodding knowingly, as though I've just delivered a dark and unrepeatable confession. As though "She's four years old" has told her more than she would ever need to know (like the fact that, earlier today, while trying to show me her new pill-bug pet, my daughter slammed her palm into my face and gave me a bloody nose, for example).

Millie leans over and whispers, "I don't usually do this. The little ones don't like it so much."

"Do what?" I ask.

Millie doesn't answer; she just lays her fingers on my head and begins to massage it. Actually, not so much massage my head as assault it. She must have at some point in her life milked cows full-time, because this woman has the finger strength of fifteen dairy farmers. Of course the young ones don't like this—no child's skull could withstand this kind of force; their heads would literally explode into puffs of confetti—but me, I simply surrender to the awesome power of Millie's man-hands, resisting the urge to cry while she squeezes my temples as though she is trying to get her fingers to touch somewhere in the middle.

As I close my eyes and give myself over to Millie's massausage fingers, memories begin flooding in—like the time I was fourteen and my friend's sister took us to see a Chippendale's show, and when one of the dancers came into the audience to hand out flowers, I gave him a dollar and tried to French-kiss the poor, frightened, nearly nude man . . . Dear Lord, I haven't thought about that in years. What's happening? Am I lucid dreaming? Having a stroke? Am I high? Or is it possible that Millie just touched my soul?

I open my eyes to see Millie now holding a large pair of scissors (regular, not pinking). She gives me a once-over.

"Not too short? Just trim?" she asks.

I nod, cross-eyed, unable to form even a word, and vaguely aware of the bad mood I came in with. What was I mad about exactly? It was important, wasn't it? Oh, yeah. My hand. The list. This place. That kid. I'm still mad about all those things . . . right?

Millie begins to cut my hair, quickly and deftly, fluttering in circles around me with the grace of Baryshnikov, if he were a 200-pound, sixty-five-year-old woman from an indeterminate eastern European country. She stops in front of me and begins to chisel away at my bangs like a sculptor, leaving me for a disturbingly long time at eye level with her terrifying chest, its cleavage so impossibly deep it seems she could store legal-size folders in there, maybe even a credit card reader.

I ask Millie—as much to confirm that I still have the ability to speak as anything else—"So . . . do you like working here?"

"Is good," she says. "I was working before at downtown salon. I had lady who ask me to make her look like Halle

Berry. She was seventy-eight-year-old white woman. I say, I want also to look like Halle Berry. I would like also for my husband not be fekking the landlady, but you know we do not live in fantasy land."

I am caught so off-guard by this admission that I reflexively reach for my neck like an elderly southern lady clutching at her pearls.

"Oh! And so . . . So then you came to work here?"

"After I am fired, yes. I like it very much."

"You like working with children?" I ask.

She nods. "They dun't complain. Sometimes they cry, or make peess in their pants, but only because they are scared. I like the difficult ones, the ones who make tantrums. I tell them I am witch. When they ask if I am good witch, I say, 'What do you think?' They dun't cry after that."

Millie lowers her voice and leans in to my ear. "My extra-special ones," she whispers, "sometimes I let them under wig to see." Then she adjusts her own hair by about 45 degrees. This causes me to flinch, which I then attempt to cover with a brief coughing fit.

"Do you—do you have kids?" I ask.

She is quiet for a moment, with a silence that speaks volumes. Perhaps her children have died. Or maybe she couldn't have any. Whatever the reason, it makes me want to hold her—

"My son drop out of law school to be rapper. My daughter is on third husband. Such disappointments." She sprays the air with Kool-Aid mist as if to cleanse it of their memory.

Suddenly, CAITLIN! comes over. As Millie turns, I catch the glint of something shiny poking out of her brassiere—perhaps it's a section of overburdened underwire gone AWOL? Or maybe it's the edge of a flask? Or a KGB-issued 9mm Makarov semiautomatic pistol? She moves too fast for me to be sure of anything.

Meanwhile, CAITLIN! whispers something to Millie, who grunt-responds, "*Mmh mmh mmh,*" and then whispers something back. Caitlin nods. Have I just witnessed a hit being ordered on someone's life? Or has some little kid plugged the toilet in the back? Rationally, I know that I'm letting my imagination get carried away. But still, my mouth goes dry at the possibilities.

Millie, still talk-grunting with CAITLIN! reaches into her smock pocket, pulls out a purple lollipop, lays it on my lap, and flashes a knowing smile my way. Is she reading my thoughts? How else could she know the dryness level of my mouth? Or that purple is my favorite flavor? I feel like I've just entered *The Matrix,* and I don't know what's real anymore.

But what's weirder is, I like it.

The door to the salon opens, and a little boy, maybe three years old, runs in. He throws himself at Millie and hugs her leg. She ruffles his hair.

"My Brrrrayden!"

Brayden glares at me—I am clearly in *his* chair. He sees, then reaches for, my lolly, where Millie left it on top of my smock. I grab it—and Brayden's hand—through the nylon material. Brayden's eyes widen in terror. Good, I think. Be afraid. And back off, kid—I ain't done yet.

Millie pats him on the head. "Go sit. Is almost time." Brayden gives me a dirty look and slinks off to sit at the bench that I hope is still just a little bit thigh-sticky.

Meanwhile, my daughter—oh, right, I have a daughter—calls to me from across the reality chasm, her hair a bouncy halo of monstrous, sparkly curls.

"MA-MA, LOOK!"

I smile as she bounds over, reaching into my purse for a crumpled fiver, which I then shove into her hand before sending her off in the direction of the Claw Grabber Game. I don't know what Millie did to me—whether she used some form of gypsy voodoo black magic, or if maybe she just jammed her scissors up my nose when I wasn't looking and gave me a quick lobotomy. All I know is that I would give my daughter the password to my ATM card right now if it would get me an extra two minutes in the eye of Millie's sweat-cloud.

Millie spins me around to the mirror to show me her handiwork.

Although it's not the worst haircut I've ever had, it's definitely far from the best. The most I can say about it is that it's level.

I nod as if to say, "It looks amazing." * Millie grunts a gracious, "*Mmh mmh mmh,*" as if to say, "You're welcome." I lean in to her gargantuan bosom, wishing I could stay just a little longer. But of course, I can't. She pats my head while I pop the purple lolly into my mouth, and then she pulls away. Oh, Millie, you wicked enchantress, you.

---

*Which, just to reiterate, it doesn't.

I step out of the chair and tip her (big), and as she sweeps up my hairs a thought occurs to me. "Millie," I ask, "when you said you like the difficult ones—were you talking about me?"

She picks something green out of her teeth and looks at it, then at me. "What do you think?" Then she pulls her wig up and gives me a quick peek at her wispy bald dome underneath. And damn it all if the sight doesn't give me a huge thrill.

I grab my daughter, the volume of her six-inch-high hairdo equal to the volume of useless plastic booty that she's extracted from the Claw Grabber Game. We head for the cashier, passing the toddler who is still *BLAPATTA-BLAPATTA*'ing away on Strawberry Short-cake's paddles. Through my new, Millie-improved eyes, I begin to believe that he may have some innate talent for pinball after all.

As CAITLIN! rings us up, she asks, "SO, PRIN-CESSES, DID YOU HAVE A MAGICAL DAY?!" And as much as I hate being proven wrong—and believe me, I do—for once I am grateful for it. OH EM GEE, CAITLIN! IT HAS BEEN A MAGICAL DAY!

seventeen

WAYS IN WHICH MY PRESCHOOLER HAS INSULTED ME

MOMMY, WHEN YOU MOVE YOUR ARMS REALLY FAST, SOMETIMES IT SOUNDS LIKE YOU'RE CLAPPING • CAMPBELL'S MOM IS SO MUCH PRETTIER THAN YOU. AND FUN-NER. AND NICER. BUT YOU'RE BETTER AT FOLDING THINGS • MOMMY, YOUR TUMMY LOOKS LIKE A BAGEL • DON'T SING ANYMORE, MOMMY. IT MAKES MY EARS SAD • WHEN WE GET HOME I'LL TELL YOU ALL THE THINGS YOU DID WRONG TODAY, MOMMY • WHAT ELSE DON'T YOU KNOW? • OW, MOMMY, YOUR FEET ARE TOO SCRATCHY! • MOMMY, ARE YOU GOING TO MAKE YOURSELF PRETTY TODAY, OR

ARE YOU GOING TO LOOK LIKE YOU ALWAYS DO?
• WHY DO YOU LOOK LIKE A DINOSAUR WHEN
YOU DANCE? • SOMETIMES YOUR MAD FACE
MAKES ME LAUGH • IS DADDY COMING HOME
SOON? YOU'RE BORING • MOMMY, DID YOU TAKE
A SHOWER TODAY? BECAUSE I DON'T THINK IT
WORKED • MOMMY, CAN I HAVE YOUR IPAD WHEN
YOU DIE? • SOMETIMES WHEN YOU KISS ME YOUR
TEETH SMELL LIKE SOCKS • MOMMY, YOUR BUTT
IS JIGGLY LIKE JELLY. AND ALSO LIKE JELLO • YOU
HAVE A LOT OF HAIRS ON YOUR FACE. IS THAT
A MUSTACHE OR A BEARD? • I WANT DADDY TO
READ MY BEDTIME STORY. HE READS IT BET-
TER AND HE DOESN'T TALK SO LOUD • CLARA
AND I WERE PLAYING IN YOUR UNDERPANTS.
THEY FIT BOTH OF US AT THE SAME TIME, HA
HA! • THE HAIR ON YOUR LEGS REMINDS ME OF
A DANDELION. THE FURRY KIND YOU BLOW ON
• WHY DO YOU HAVE ALL THOSE MEAN LINES
ON YOUR FACE? • WHICH ONE IS THE OLDEST:
GRANDMA, GRANDPA, OR YOU? • AUGH!! YOU
SCARED ME. YOUR FACE LOOKED LIKE AN ALIEN
• IT'S SO FUNNY HOW THE HAIR ON YOUR KIKI
LOOKS LIKE A SQUIRREL'S TAIL • WHEN YOU DIE
CAN I ALSO HAVE YOUR WEDDING RING? • YOUR
BREATH SMELLS LIKE A FART.

eighteen

MY VERY AMERICAN GIRL

"MOMMY, YOU'RE GOING TOO FAST."

It's eight o'clock on a Saturday morning. We are speed-walking to a yard sale that I've been planning to hit since last night when I'd pulled the flier off a telephone pole and committed the address to memory before using it to pick up a piece of my dog's Tootsie Roll–size poo.

Honoring my daughter's request, I slow my pace, though this is difficult for me—like holding back a jaguar about to pounce upon an injured fawn. The quest for bargains falls somewhere between sport and religion for me. I take after my mom in this regard—and I say this with deep respect for the woman who has given me food poisoning more than once because of her insistence on keeping food long past the "fresh by" date.

The fact is, I love my shopping like I like my men: cheap, easy, and accessible by car. . . . But mostly just cheap. I once bought sixteen boxes of tampons at the corner store because they were discounted by 75 percent. Why they were so heavily marked down, I have no idea, but if you'd told me it was because they were "pre-owned," it wouldn't have made a difference to me: I am all about the bargain, and the bragging rights that follow.

Yard sales occupy a special place in my heart—not only are they like snowflakes in their uniqueness, they offer the added thrill of the chase. It's elemental; man versus man, Haggler versus Hag. The argument could even be made that I am borderline ruthless in my pursuit of the perfect deal; I once came very close to wounding a woman over a yard-sale fondue pot. I had just picked it up to inspect it when she yelled to the owner, "HOW MUCH YOU WANT FOR THAT?" as though the volume of her desperate request trumped my "possession is nine-tenths of the law" status. I was so enraged I nearly stabbed her with one of the still faintly cheesy-smelling skewers; instead, I regained my composure, hissed a "thanks" at her for brokering my deal, and then sauntered away, one Three-Dollar Fondue Pot richer.

I am the Queen of the Crap That You No Longer Want or Need. And on this Saturday morning I am salivating at the thought of sharing—and eventually handing off—the glorious crown to my four-year-old daughter.

As we walk up the cracked driveway, a sea of treasures spreads out before us, and my heartbeat quickens with the potential of what we might find.

I am making a quick and thorough visual scan of the goods (men's clothes, garden tools, a poorly collaged mirror, stained luggage) when I see the seller: a sixtyish woman poured into a yellow "Juicy" tracksuit, a hot-pink fanny pack bisecting her middle, and on her head a nest of orange curly hair just barely contained by a "Las Vegas Is for Lovers" visor. The sight of this woman at so early an hour makes my corneas ache.

She is in midhaggle with a young couple over a dingy, busted-up wicker armchair. "Can I give you twenty dollars?" the man asks.

"I paid over a thousand dollars for that new in 1983," she drawls. "All it needs is to be recaned, reglued, restuffed, and upholstered. And you want me to give it away for twenty dollars? No, sir! One fifty's the lowest I can go."

This isn't haggling; this is delusional price-setting, a cardinal sin among yard salers. Clearly, her overenthusiastic use of chemical hair dye has obliterated her common sense. We will not score here—it is time to cut bait.

I grab my daughter's hand. "Doesn't look like they have anything we need. Let's go home for waffles!"

The Vegas-loving eyesore steps in front of my daughter: "What a sweet pea! I bet I've got something you'd like!" And before I can process what is about to happen, she flexes her sausage-cased arms and opens a suitcase to reveal a disheveled doll who smiles blankly, oblivious to the shit storm that she is about to unleash.

A sweat mustache begins to form on my lip. I try to steer my child away, but I can see by her wide-eyed expression that I am too late.

"That's an American Girl doll," the woman says. "They're a hundred dollars new, y'know."

No lady, I didn't know that. I live underground, I have never seen a TV, nor have I heard of computers, condoms, or penicillin. Of course I know the price of an American Girl doll. I'm a mother to a four-year-old female and have been trying to shield her from this specter of marketing genius since the moment the doctor said, "There's one lip, and there's the other lip. It's a girl!"

⚮

When I was a kid we had Barbie. With her Dolly Parton figure and Farrah Fawcett smile, she was like nicotine to our little lady brains.

My Barbie collection was small, but impressive enough to have been stolen sometime around my tenth birthday (a fact that enrages me to this day). And though I did not possess the holy grail of Barbie products—Barbie's glorious Camper Van—the crowning glory of my collection was a "Growing Up Skipper" doll. With a 360-degree spin of her arm, she would grow an inch taller from the torso, and two conical protrusions would fill out her pliable rubber chest, turning this adorable little girl into a fully pubescent young lady. (A curious feature of Growing Up Skipper was that, after a few months, the rubber on her chest hardened to a state of permanent breast-iosity, leaving young Skipper looking like a disturbingly well-stacked eight-year-old.)

But as much as I loved my Barbies, they are mere candy cigarettes compared to the crack cocaine of American Girl dolls today.

∿

My daughter fell for her first American Girl when she was two and a half years old, and may God have mercy on me, it was my own damn fault.

We were living in Chicago at the time and taking a walk downtown on what turned out to be a balmy, thirty-below-zero winter day. So as not to perish, we sought refuge in the nearest heated building, which was the American Girl flagship store.

We'd been there countless times before—it was a frequent shortcut due to its convenient location and hassle-free bathrooms, and I have to admit, as I pushed my disinterested toddler's stroller through the aisles, I got a chuckle at the sight of tween girls crying and being scolded by their mothers "BECAUSE YOU'VE ALREADY GOT SIX DOLLS, THAT'S WHY!"

I laughed because I thought we were safe. I thought we were immune.

I thought oh-so-cockily wrong.

By the time I'd pulled the ice-encrusted scarf away from my daughter's face, I could tell that something in her had been stirred, as though a second set of eyelids had been peeled back from her eyes and she was finally, for the first time in her short life, truly awake.

She sat straight up, cocked her head, and then stretched her sticky, chubby hands toward an immaculate display filled with dolls of every eye, hair, and skin color—each one wearing a vacant expression that seemed to be chanting, "One of us! One of us!"

My kid opened her mouth and began to scream/chant/gurgle, "MAAAHHH! MAAAHHH!" Whether she was trying to say, "Mine!" or "MOM!" or whether it was just a primal sound emanating from deep within her soul, I can't say, because I ran that stroller out of there at a speed far faster than would have been safe, like all those other moms I'd laughed at not so very long ago.

My days became a series of evasion tactics: avoiding the store (two blocks from our home), intercepting the mail carrier before he could deliver the American Girl catalog, and crossing the street to avoid the neighborhood twin girls who carried twin American Girl versions of themselves everywhere they went (a disturbing and creepy sight).

Then came the repeated requests from the child, with an alarming frequency:

"I HAVE AN AMERICAN DOLL?" "Someday, sure."

"I HAVE AN AMERICAN DOLL?" "Someday, yes."

"I HAVE AN AMERICAN DOLL?" "Someday, okay."

And yes, deep down I meant it, though I may have left out the "maybe after a nuclear holocaust" part. Because you know what? I never got a Barbie Camper Van, and I turned out okay. Sort of.

⤳

The American Girl store is a marvel of retail success. It has three beautifully appointed stories of merchandise. There's a café where little girls can enjoy high-priced tea with their dolls and captive grandparents. There's a dolly hair salon, and an actual dolly hospital where the healthcare services rival anything available through my own HMO. As a proud member of our capitalist culture, I am both inspired and impressed by the success of this business.

But as a parent and lifelong bargain hunter, I am offended to my very core by everything it stands for. Most offensive is that, as of this writing, a new doll costs over one hundred bones, more than I have ever paid for a regular article of clothing and only slightly less than I paid for my wedding dress. One hundred dollars for a child's toy that doesn't even plug in? Not my bag, baby. And definitely not the knock-off bag that has been passed down to me by my mother.

And now here I am, standing at the edge of a lesson in bargain hunting. Seems I will be going into battle after all.

⚘

"Yes," I say to my neon-clad rival, "there's quite a market for these dolls . . . when they're in good condition. This one looks like it was well loved. By an aggressive, long-haired cat."

One cool hand, casually played.

The Velour Demoness smiles at me. "It belonged to my daughter, Debi. She's on her way to Princeton this year on a tennis scholarship."

Ooh, she is good, implying that the doll's got Ivy League juju all over it. But I don't care if this doll comes with a transferable master's degree. I will not pay more than ten dollars for it.

Me: "I'll give you five dollars."

One low-ball gauntlet, forcefully thrown down.

Old Juicy Dusty-Buns makes a sound like a cat coughing up a hair ball and says with disgust, "I can't take less than twenty-five."

And here's where I pull my signature move: the laugh/walk-away combo that I'm guessing should result in a decent counteroffer, maybe fifteen dollars.

But the Orange-Haloed Battle-Ax does not quake under my laissez-faire attitude. Instead, she shakes her head and hisses as she sets the doll back into the suitcase.

She is tough as nails—she's not budging. Well, neither am I. I grab my kid's hand and start to walk away. I give her a sly wink, my attempt to show her that this is all part of the dance, but at four years old she doesn't understand subtlety or the machinations of yard-sale subterfuge, the art that I learned at my mother's knee and have perfected over twenty years of professional cheapskate-ism.

Her chin begins to quiver. "WHY I CAN'T HAVE THE AMERICAN DOLL?"

We are knee-deep in a teachable moment—but what will it teach her? Will it be a lesson in standing up for your principles, regardless of the outcome—or will it be a lesson in "you can't always get what you want"? Or maybe it will be a lesson in how easily Mommy loses sight of her priorities. Or how wide Mommy's nostrils flare when she's agitated and backed into a corner.

I don't like corners like this, particularly corners that break another cardinal rule of yard-sale-ing—never haggle over something that you are not prepared to lose.

I should walk, but I don't.

"I'll give you seven dollars."

"Twenty-five."

"Eight."

"Twenty-five."

"Nine dollars and 75 cents." (I immediately regret the seventy-five-cents maneuver—it reeks of desperation.)

"Twenty-five."

Another laugh (hers), another turn/walk (mine). This one not so much a tactic as a time stall.

I mumble to my opponent that I'm going to take a look around and see what else she's got.

My mind races as I scan the yard: a threadbare cowboy hat . . . a salad spinner . . . faded Mickey Mouse ears . . . lederhosen (lederhosen?!) . . . and a cracked replica of a samurai sword, which is beginning to look more and more useful as the minutes pass.

I look at my daughter, now cradling the frizzy-haired doll with an ink-stained foot and one lazy eye, stroking its face and whispering into its ear, and God help me I watch as my hand, now seemingly possessed, reaches into my purse and pulls out a twenty-dollar bill and five bucks in change, then hands it to the Goldenrod-Haired Gargoyle, who smiles in victory.

Because this is what happens when theory meets reality. When principles meet real life. When your deeply held beliefs meet the gaze of your four-year-old's pleading eyes.

"ENJOY!" shrieks the Hideous Victor Who Has Stolen My Mantle of Yard Sale Supremacy and then turns her attention to an elderly man testing out a rusty wheelchair that's missing two front wheels. "You take off the other two wheels and you've got an office chair that's better for your back than anything you could buy at Staples. I'll let you have it for ninety dollars."

My daughter scrutinizes the doll as though she cannot fathom what she is seeing with her own eyes. She looks back at me in the same way.

On the walk home, as if to twist the knife, the kid talks about all of the things we're going to have to buy for her new (pre-owned!) American Girl doll—the clothes, accessories, visits to the café, and the friggin salon—because this used doll, for which I paid way too much, BTW, is just the gateway drug. I see now that I have failed my cheapskate self in more ways than one.

I tune out the child to say a small, silent prayer that, like every other toy in the history of her, she'll lose interest in it after ten minutes.

↝

The child does not put the doll down for the rest of the day. She goes to sleep, holding it tightly, like a motherless rhesus monkey.

When she is finally asleep, I sneak back into her room to inspect the toy; so help me if I find one mite or spider on it, I will walk straight to that woman's house, set fire to the doll's hair, and lob it through her bedroom window.

I gently pry the doll from my daughter's arm. It's heavier and more substantial than I'd imagined—and I take it into the bathroom, where I give it a wipe-down with a wet washcloth. The pen mark comes right off the foot, the toes of which are very detailed, it turns out. Giving it a once-over, I verify that all the parts are in working order. The arms and legs rotate as they should, and I manage to work the shut eye open, though it still blinks a little slowly, like maybe she's winking because she thinks she pulled a fast one on me.

I take the doll into the living room, where I go to work on her hair, brushing carefully from the bottom and working up so as not to pull out too many strands. Looking closely at her face, I realize I hadn't noticed before the little space between her teeth, or the tiny gold hoop earrings encircling her little earlobes.

The hair is now untangled, but I keep brushing until it is glossy and smooth to the touch. It's so soft—now I'm just stroking her hair, marveling at how nice it feels against my hand.

My husband walks past and looks at me funny. "Get a room," he says and then laughs loudly at his own joke as he goes to the fridge for a snack. "Good one," I think but don't say. (If I gave him every laugh he deserved, he'd be unbearable.)

I pull the doll close to my face and lay my cheek on it. She smells of nylon and toy plastic. It's a sickeningly sweet, industrial smell, and it opens the curtains wide on my own childhood memories and of countless toys I've loved and coveted from afar.

I understand this doll. I like this doll. I want this doll. I—

"MAMA?"

I turn to see my daughter looking at me, sleepy be-trayal on her face.

"WHY DID YOU TAKE MY AMERICAN DOLL, MAMA?"

"I—I was just cleaning her for you." I say, not very convincingly. I hand over the doll—though not easily—and send the child back to bed. She walks sleepily up-stairs, accidentally bonking its freshly brushed head on the banister. I make a note to take it to the American Girl salon one afternoon while the kid is at school. Maybe I'll even grab myself a seven-dollar coffee at the café while the doll gets her hair styled to the tune of forty dollars. Because sometimes we turn into our mothers. And some-times we turn into our daughters.

✤ nineteen ✤

THE FIRST BABY

The child was in deep mourning for the Chicago Cubs. After a four-year stint in Chicago we moved back to Los Angeles, and the kid was torn with grief. I'd wake up at two o clock in the morning to find her standing next to our bed, cradling a giant foam finger and sobbing, "I MISS THE CUBBIEEZ!" At four years old, I figured, she wasn't pining for Chicago's losingest professional baseball team so much as she was grieving the personal loss of their concessions stand. But that didn't make her grief any less real, because it doesn't matter how old you are, the heart wants what the heart wants, i.e., Wrigley Field hot dogs and bags of cotton candy the size of a grown man's head.

In lieu of picking up our lives and moving all the way back to Chicago just for the ballpark snacks, we considered the next most obvious solution: we would get a dog. Because if I've learned one thing in life, it's that nothing soothes change and upheaval like a shitload more upheaval and change.

We decided to let the kid choose from a group of pre-approved-by-me dogs. I'd clicked through a nice array of candidates posted on the local Humane Society's website; one of the featured dogs was a small black mutt that looked like what you might end up with if you were to peel the face off a human boy and staple it onto the body of a Pomeranian. Of course I put Dogboy on the short list and then headed over to the shelter to interview him and a few other possibilities.

Once there I narrowed it down to three contenders: an apparently stoned shih tzu, an incontinent Maltese, and Dogboy (who wasn't quite so weird-looking in person, much to my disappointment), which is when the husband brought the kid in to make her selection.

The kid picked Dogboy.

Dogboy turned out to be a good dog (boy), especially after he got past his credit-card-and-couch-eating phase. He was attentive, sweet tempered, and well behaved. But good as he was, Dogboy was at a huge disadvantage coming into our family. He didn't know it, but he had some very big paw prints to fill.

⮞⮜

It was 1994. I'd been in L.A. for just over a year and had lived through riots, fires, and a robbery/shooting in my front yard, all of which left me feeling that the city was one long amusement-park ride with a bad record of safety violations.

It was three o'clock in the morning, and I was awake, watching a bad reality show, at a time when "bad reality show" had not yet proved redundant.

My roommate was in France for the winter, and so when the floor began to roll and the cupboards began to vibrate and the vacuum cleaner leaped out of the pantry, there was no one to witness the sight of me leaping naked into my bedroom doorway where, just as the thought "so this is where it all ends" crossed my synapses, my ovaries commanded EVACUATE! and I spontaneously started my period and proceeded to bleed all over the rolling floor.

I didn't die in the Northridge earthquake. I lived to see the next day, and after some cleaning up of broken dishes and stained carpets, I had one of those epiphanies you have when you make it to other side of a near-death experience, and it had clarified two things for me: (1) if/when the world was going to end, I didn't want to be alone; and (2) Los Angeles is no place to be sleeping in the nude.

I toyed briefly with the idea of having a baby,* but as my romantic/fertilization prospects were less than ideal (i.e., I was half-dating a guy whose idea of foreplay was a forty-five-minute conversation about how much his foot resembled William Shatner), I settled on the next best thing. I would get a dog.

---

*Because isn't that how all normal people react to a natural disaster?

I'd never had a dog before—the closest I'd ever gotten was when I was a kid and my dad would fling open the front door and yell "SCREW YOU!" at the neighbor's German shepherd as it frolicked in our yard, gleefully covering it with lawn bombs.

When I ran the idea up the flagpoles of my friends, I was surprised at how many of them disapproved. They showered me with such warnings as:

"You'll lose your spontaneity."	*True, I won't be able to jet off to Paris at the drop of a hat, but that doesn't seem to be an issue considering that, for me, a big night out means a meatball dinner at IKEA.*
"A dog will make your apartment smell."	*Perhaps. But worse than it already does? Doubtful.*
"You'll become one of those creepy women that French-kisses her dog."	*You say that like it's a bad thing.*
"It'll tear your throat out while you sleep."	*Good point: I'll stock up on turtleneck negligees.*

Their arguments notwithstanding, I refused to be dissuaded.

I visited shelters, scoured local ads, and petted my way through dog adoption events. In a moment of alcohol-induced spirituality, I determined that the winning applicant would be the first dog who responded to one of the five following names: Sparky, Lucky, Eddie, Sam, and Donut (I was secretly praying, of course, for a Donut).

Then I found a listing for a young rescued Dalmatian that sounded suspiciously like it might be a Donut. I phoned the dog rescuer, a woman named Maude, who proved to be, like 99.25 percent of dog rescuers in this world, kind, caring, and certifiably insane. No matter, I figured, I'm an experienced and dedicated suck-up from way back; as a kid, there wasn't a teacher or parent alive I couldn't win over.

Maude told me how she'd come to find "Spot" wandering, collarless, in a park that she frequents with her metal-detecting group ("The Heavy Metals") and that he was house trained, healthy, and playful. Maude and I had been enjoying a pleasant conversation for nearly thirty minutes—me sharing details of my daily work schedule and prior pet experience, her sharing details of how alien abduction proves the existence of reincarnation—when Maude stopped me midsentence and said, "I've just had a sensation. This is not the dog for you."

"Wait—what do you mean? Was it something I said—?"

"Sorry. This is not going to work." Click. Dial tone.

I looked around the empty living room for someone to validate my horror at being so harshly rejected, then realized this would have been an ideal moment to share with a dog with expressive eyebrows.

Forty minutes later the phone rang. It was Maude.

"I have another dog for you. I'm coming over."

"Now?" It was ten thirty at night. I was already in my pajamas (as I said, I wasn't taking any more chances with disaster-induced streaking).

"Tomorrow morning. I'll be there at seven. With Spot." She paused. "Not the same Spot. A different one." Click. Dial tone.

Seven o'clock the next morning the doorbell rang.

I opened the door to a burly woman with piercing eyes and a grave expression, and immediately I recognized the error of my ways: Maude was no dog rescuer. She was a serial killer who preyed on wannabe dog owners. Our thirty-minute phone interview last night had given her everything she needed to know—it would be easy for her to kill me and cover her tracks. My friends had been right—getting a dog was a dumb idea, and now I was going to die for it.

"You Johanna? I'll get Spot."

I watched as Maude walked back to her dust-covered Volvo, reached in, pulled out a small armload of fur, and then came into my apartment and set it on the floor.

I sat cross-legged on the carpet so as to get a good, close look at the mutt. He looked like maybe he was part terrier. Black and white, with spots, like a Holstein cow. Fifteen pounds, give or take. And a face covered with wiry, scruffy hair, topped by a set of unruly, Abe Vigoda–esque eyebrows.

The dog trotted over to me, stared me up and down, turned his back to me, and sat on my lap.

Though it seemed he'd already made his decision, I wanted at least the illusion of having a say in the matter, so I ran through my List of Five: "Sparky? . . . Lucky? . . . Eddie? . . ." He turned and looked me in the eyes. "Donut? . . ." He looked away. I went through the List of Five one more time, trying hard to get him to respond to Donut, but there was no question—Spot was an Eddie.

I thanked Maude, the non-serial-killing (as far as I knew, anyway) dog rescuer, and set out to bond with my new dog/surrogate baby/life enhancer.

Eddie was cool, slightly indignant, and somewhat intense—a cross between Charlie Sheen and Marlon Brando; like any minute he might lift a leg and pee on a wall, but if he did you'd know he probably had a good reason for it. I imagined that he was a tiny man in a dog suit, and that, late at night, he'd unzip himself and take long rides along the coast on a tiny Harley with no helmet, and a teeny unlit cigarette hanging out the side of his kibble-smelling mouth.

Eddie had a good sense of humor and an impeccable sense of timing. During our first week together, I took him to the beach. He trotted over to a group of thong-wearing sunbathing twenty-somethings and peed on the one with the biggest boobs.

When sirens wailed in the neighborhood, Eddie howled back dramatically, but not with the full-throated majesty of a wolf; he sounded more like a twelve-year-old boy whose voice was on the verge of cracking. It made me laugh till I cried, the way he turned strangers' tragedies into my personal amusement.

Eddie was smart and picked up commands easily. If you asked, "Are you the queen?" he'd delicately place his paw in your hand. And if you shot him with your finger gun and said "KAPOW," he'd enact a long, slow death scene, laying down ever so gently on his back, sticking his paws in the air, and then looking sideways at you with a pitiful expression on his fake-dying face.

He was not a licker; he would not stoop to such obvious pandering. Instead, he liked to cart my shoes around—not chew them, just carry them around in his mouth like some weird IT guy with a foot fetish. On days that I was late for work, running around the house with five mismatched shoes in hand could get annoying, but mostly I just found it flattering.

Eddie wasn't perfect—he barked ferociously at tall men with dark complexions. And on top of his racist leanings, he was known to hump—never humans, only other dogs (usually in the ear), and very occasionally unsuspecting inanimate objects. I was not a fan of the way his lipstick would unfurl at those times; nor was I fan of the way he'd occasionally drag his anus along the carpet and smile seductively as he did—not that I could blame him, as I imagine the feeling must have been heavenly.

But Eddie's imperfections did not repel me; they just endeared him to me as we made our way hand-in-paw through roommates, apartments, jobs, and friends. Through ups, downs, and way-the-hell-deep-downs. And boyfriends. Lots and lots and lots of those. Because through it all, Eddie was family. He was my baby.

When I brought home the guy who would eventually become the husband, I was nervous that he wouldn't take to Eddie. But he did, even after Eddie created a flea infestation in his apartment that required a two-day evacuation. And though I worried that Eddie wouldn't take to the guy, he did. So well, in fact, there were times I'd enter a room to see Eddie laying in his lap, gazing up into his eyes, and clearly thinking, "Oh, how I wish that I were a woman."

Even after we got married, Eddie retained a place of honor in our home. He slept in bed with us and developed the polite habit of jumping onto the floor and sequestering himself in the closet whenever the bed started to get a little too bouncy for his liking.

By the time I got knocked up, Eddie was a spry twelve years old—and as essential to me as my right arm, or that woman who shaves the dry skin off my heels once a year.

But friends shook their heads knowingly. "You'll see," they'd say. "Once that baby comes, it won't be the same. He'll fall down the priority list. He won't be your baby anymore—he'll just be a dog."

"How dare they!" I'd say to myself. They don't know us. They don't know how strong our bond is. They don't know that sometimes, often after a glass or two of wine, I start to believe that Eddie's communicating with me telepathically. (And yes, I realize how crazy that sounds, which is probably why I only ever said it to myself.)

Still, for Eddie's sake, we prepared for the transition, doing everything the books tell you to do. We showered him with treats and extra-long walks—and when he got tired on those walks, I'd carry him in my arms, like Dickens's Tiny Tim. We got him a special dog bed for the baby's room and didn't even color coordinate it to match her room, because screw the baby—Eddie was a winter and his color was red.

On the day we checked into the hospital, Eddie stayed with a friend. As we drove home two days later with our new human, I was nervous and unsure. Would Eddie attempt to eat the baby? Hump her? Urinate on her and mark her as his territory?

When we walked in the door I brought the sleeping baby down to his level so that he could get a sniff—making sure not to get too close just in case he chose that moment to lose his mind and try to rip out her brand-spanking-new throat.

Eddie didn't rip out her throat. He didn't even look at her. He just stared into my eyes and then walked past us and into our bedroom, where he flopped down on the rug. He wouldn't even acknowledge the child's existence. It was beyond disdain. It was as though he was experiencing some sort of rare mental disease ("Baby Blindness") that Oliver Sacks might write about.

And that's how it went. For weeks. I thought that maybe this was some manipulative ploy of his and that one morning we would walk into the baby's room to find her gone, replaced with a replica of her made entirely from kibble. But no, Eddie just continued his tactic of baby ignoring. Until one day, sometime in her eighth month, she spastically reached for his tail and caught it—and he growled at her. I, of course, lost my shit on him like Shirley MacLaine (crossed with a three-headed Hydra) screaming at the nurse in *Terms of Endearment*. Eddie cowered and shivered. And then he crept toward me, licked my hand—and then he licked the baby.

I felt horrible about how I'd lost my cool. But Eddie didn't hold a grudge, and from that moment on, his attitude changed. Perhaps it was his survivor's memory, or maybe it was because it happened around the time she began handling food and dropping pounds of it daily on the floor below her high chair, but almost immediately he began sleeping in her room.

It was also around that time that Eddie developed a loud, phlegmy hack, like some old guy at a bus stop trying to cough out a lung.

At first I thought Eddie was just being dramatic and trying to horn in on all the attention the baby was getting. Then he started urinating in strange and random spots in the house, like a confused, drunk teenager pissing into his gym bag, convinced that it's a urinal. The vet diagnosed him with an enlarged heart and wondered did we want to put him on some medication, the side effects of which could include incontinence, drowsiness, orneriness, and a whole list of other -nesses of the unpleasant sort.

The husband and I agreed we didn't want to drag Eddie through endless procedures and treatments. So we decided that we'd just try to make the rest of his life comfortable, however long that might be. And besides, I figured, the best-case scenario would be if his heart just continued to grow, up to the point that he simply dropped dead of a heart attack, preferably with his face in one of my shoes.

Then that cross-country move from Los Angeles to Chicago in the dead of winter presented itself, and we took it. We worried the change might kill our old, hacky, incontinent dog. Not only did it not kill him, but damn it all if that old bugger didn't catch himself a second wind.

The first time we took a walk to the shore of Lake Michigan, we watched with gaping mouths and puffs of steam pouring out of them as this suddenly frisky senior-citizen dog began goofily frolicking in the deep snow with our equally goofy year-old baby.

It seemed surprising yet totally inevitable that our dog would be so inspired by this late-life change. He even picked up his humping habits with renewed vigor, focusing his romantic interests on a St. Bernard puppy who lived in the apartment next door.

Then, four months after moving to Chicago, we left Eddie with a friend while we buzzed out of town for a quick weekend with the in-laws. On the second day the dog sitter called. She was in hysterics.

"Slow down, I can't hear you . . . "

"EDDIE'S DEAD! HE'S DEAD!"

Slipping into my control-freak default position, I assumed she must be wrong. "Hang on. Are you *sure* he's dead?"

She was sure, she sobbed. She'd gone out to the store and had come home to find Eddie on the floor in the living room, dead, with his head not in my shoes but in a box of Triscuits.

The little bastard, he died like he lived. On his own terms, and with snacks.

He was fourteen years old.

Though there wasn't any real urgency as (a) Eddie was waiting for us in the vet's freezer, and (b) he wasn't going to get any more dead than he already was, we cut our trip short and returned home immediately. It just seemed wrong to leave him stuck on ice next to some unworthy, shitty cat.

At the vet's office a technician pulled Eddie out of the freezer and dropped him onto the counter, then gave us his condolences and shut the door behind him. Eddie looked surprisingly good for a dead dog, just a pink petrified tongue sticking out the side of his mouth giving any indication as to his permanent state of deadness. We petted and hugged our beautiful dead doggie-pop, with our snotty tears setting onto his ice-cold fur, and the knowledge that if he were alive, he'd probably be horrified by our sad, sentimental display.

I was devastated by his death. I cried and cried, and then I changed a diaper and played peek-a-boo and cut the crusts off a peanut butter sandwich, and then I cried some more. My plans to be wracked by grief and sit shivah for a week were not to be. Sure, there was time for me to lay my head and sob into Eddie's still Cheeto-smelling dog bed, but it turns out that sixteen-month-old babies have some fairly pressing needs.

Which illuminated something: now that I actually had a child, I could see quite clearly that having a dog was nothing like having a baby. Sure, they were roughly the same size, and both had figured out how to leave their fecal cleanup to the tall humans with opposable thumbs. But that's pretty much where the comparison ended. If anything, Eddie was more like a brother to me, maybe even a first husband (minus the consummation, of course).

Ours was a relationship of choice, not dependence. Eddie didn't "need" me, and there's no question that if we were to have been separated, within days he'd have been living with some Russian heiress, sitting on a pillow made of spun alpaca, eating veal treats, and having his nethers scratched from morning till night by the hired help. And in retrospect, if Eddie knew that I had ever called him my "baby," he'd probably have bitten off my left tit, just to prove a point.

So yes, maybe it's true that my relationship with my dog did change when I had a baby. But then again, so did my relationship with my husband, my parents, my friends, my work, my nipples, my body, and pretty much everything else in my life.

Now we have Dogboy, with his normal-size heart and his habit of licking our feet like the pandering perv that Eddie would have made him out to be. Though he may be no Eddie (it's not his fault, but he's not even close), Dogboy has mended the baseball-size hole that was left in the kid's heart. Sometimes I catch her playing with him in her bedroom, dressing him up in her doll's clothes, and calling him "baby brother"—which sometimes I find creepy, and other times spot-on.

twenty

ONE IS ENOUGH

I am lying on my back, feet in stirrups. Dr. V. Jay snaps on a plastic glove and gives me the old "scootch toward me." This is not how I planned on spending my Tuesday morning.

I have lived by the motto "Jump and the net will appear," and not just because I have a thing for firemen. That simple philosophy has inspired me to lead a life of frequent and deliberate change. Hairstyles, apartments, boyfriends, careers . . . I cycled through them all with the ease of an iPod shuffle.

Right now you're probably thinking, "Wow, what a flake." And you'd be right, only I prefer the term *change junkie*. It's more accurate, and besides, I kind of like the badass connotation.

But that was the old (young) me. Now I'm the new (old) me. I'm a mature (well, this point is debatable) woman; I'm a wife, with a kid, and a husband who wants another (kid, not wife). Unfortunately for him—and for three sets of eager, salivating grandparents—the concept of change now totally freaks me the freak out.

Screw that "Jump and the net will appear" crap. There could be three half-naked, six-pack-having firemen standing outside my window yelling, "Jump, you're ovulating!" and I still wouldn't budge. When it comes to this second-kid decision, I don't even have the guts to pry my body off the floor.

Let me explain: I killed at pregnancy. I was a genius at delivery. And despite my fears that I would give birth to an ugly moron, the daughter turned out to be one of the good ones (I have seen some of the bad ones, and when they go bad, it's a Thomas the Train Wreck). We're a very small, very manageable, very happy family of three. A trio. A triptych. A triangle. The strongest shape in the known universe. So why, for the love of carbs, would we push our luck? I'd always been a good gambler, and even though my experience was limited to the nickel slots in Reno, I knew when to hold 'em, when to fold 'em, when to walk away, and when to run screaming from the prospect of another kid.

But then came the vacillating. I don't know how it started, but some days I'd find my brain playing Good Cop/Crazy Cop with itself. One minute I was scheduling a vasectomy for my husband based on the fact that two out of three finalists on last season's *American Idol* were only children; the next minute I was gazing longingly at my daughter's baby pictures and telling my husband to "HURRY UP AND STICK IT IN BEFORE I CHANGE MY MIND!" Most times, though, I could fight the impulse.

And then, it happened.

Oprah happened.

It was a Sunday afternoon. The husband was out, the kid was napping, I was shaving lint balls off the couch. I turned on the TV and began watching an episode of *Oprah*, and it was a doozy. I won't go into much detail because if I do I may start crying, and until I can afford a waterproof computer I'd rather not run the risk of electrocution.

I'll just say that the topic was siblings and the lengths to which they will go to protect each other. Never mind that I grew up with two brothers whose idea of brotherly love was to fart on my head simultaneously; the episode killed me. It was as though Oprah herself had reached through the TV screen, torn my heart from my chest, had her personal chef sauté it, and then ate it with a full-bodied Bordeaux. I bawled my eyes out, heaving, sobbing, and snotting all over the place (luckily, my laptop was well out of range). When my daughter awoke from her nap, in order to quell the liquids pouring from my face I had to pinch my upper-arm flab and imagine the least pleasant thing I could think of (i.e., that time I accidentally caught a glimpse of my dad bending over in his bathrobe. PS: It worked).

My husband and I "did it" that night, the Night of the Oprah Effect. Afterward, I pulled my legs up to my chest, stuck a pillow under my rear, and tried to will the smartest of the sperm (out of the way, dum-dums!) to penetrate my lonely egg hanging out in her fallopian palace.

I awoke the next morning in a spiral of regret. "Another kid? Now? What about my career?! My time?! My life?! My boobs?! What the farg was I thinking?!"

But then I reminded myself of the odds; it had taken us well over a year to conceive the first time, so I figured chances were slim that this one would stick.

A few days later I felt an odd twinge-y/cramp-y/ PING! in my lower abdomen.

Oh no.

A wave of remorse washed over me as I remembered all the times I'd mocked those hippie chicks who claimed they could "feel" the moment of conception.

In an instant I was hit with the reality of what we had done. It was sharper and more startling than stepping on a Barbie shoe in the middle of the night. How could I have allowed Oprah to ruin everything? We'd clearly used up all our good genes on the first kid; Number Two would undoubtedly be a disaster. But not an ugly moron, no. This one would be bad. "Bad Seed" bad. Mean, nasty, wicked bad. We were nine months away and counting from Stephen King's next literary inspiration.

And then, as if to compound the emotional torture, a strange set of symptoms appeared. First up: a hot, red rash that started on my arms and then migrated across my chest and stomach. I checked in with my old doctor friend (www.webmd.com) and learned that many women experience hormonally induced hives in the beginning stages of pregnancy.

Terrific. An angry red rash: not just a pregnancy symptom, but further proof of the red-hot mistake we were making.

Then came the vertigo. If you've never felt it, vertigo is like the bed spins you felt the first time you got drunk, but without that margarita aftertaste. I'd lay awake at night clutching the bedsheets, feeling like Jimmy Stewart falling off a three-story building in *Rear Window,* only with much better special effects.

Great. So not only were we about to destroy our perfectly manageable little family setup, but I was going to spend the next nine months stumbling around in a dizzy, rashy, gassy body. (I may have neglected to mention the gassy part, as I'm not entirely certain that was a pregnancy symptom.)

The husband suggested I pick up a home pregnancy test, but it was still too early for that. Anyway, I figured, why waste the thirteen dollars? We'd need every penny since we'd soon be moving into the poorhouse. And even if we were able to keep the house, that money might come in handy when Number Two's parole officer required a bribe.

A few nights later, the most graphic proof: bright-pink spotting. I didn't even need to surf the web for this one, it had happened during my first pregnancy. This was the brightest, pinkest nail in the coffin. It was time to rewrite our future. No longer would we be the mobile, relaxed trio. Now we would be the harried, overstressed, financially unstable family of four. No more family vacations at Disney World; now we would spend holidays sorting trash at the city dump.

Still, I had to admit that even if Number Two was a disaster, it would be nice for our daughter to have someone else—a friend, a compatriot, someone to victimize, and a partner to lean on when her parents become decrepit and needy (more than we already are, anyway). And sure, her Ivy League education fund probably wouldn't be enough to cover both kids, but it would divide nicely into community college tuition for two, with enough left over for family therapy.

As I felt the boulders of long-held notions being rearranged in my mind, another unfamiliar sensation took over: a surge, as the light spotting turned into heavy spotting, and the pink turned a deep, dark red.

This was no light spotting. This was serious bleeding. Heavy, worrisome, almost like . . .

FWAP! Dr. V. Jay snaps off his plastic gloves and tosses them into a trash can.

"It's your period. A heavy one, yes, but just a period."

So what about the other symptoms? The rash? The vertigo? The uncontrollable gas?

My doctor shrugs. "I don't have an answer for you. But thank you for waiting until after the exam to tell me about the gas."

I wasn't pregnant. Not even a little. Huh.

Now you're probably thinking, "Wow, she's flaky AND has hysterical pregnancy tendencies." And again, you'd be right. But the most interesting takeaway from this story isn't the fact that I'm able to talk myself into thinking I'm pregnant (I've always been pretty persuasive); it's how relieved I don't feel at finding out that I'm not. And that "fear of change"? It's gone. Seems it's been replaced, knocked out of position by a faint sense of sadness for the little delinquent that never was, and never will be.

Which isn't to say there can't be another. Dr. V says it's true, given my age and the dustiness of my ovaries, my odds of conceiving are low and, yes, getting lower with every passing day. But, he says, if I want another, there's no reason we shouldn't keep trying.

And now I do, and so we will; we'll pull the goalie, pray for the net, and let the chips (and sperm) fall (and swim) where they may.

twenty-one

PRIVATE TIME

T he important thing to know is that we are not sex addicts.

We are not cavalier about where or when we engage in sexual congress.

We have a door on our bedroom, and we do, on occasion, close it. Because—I don't want to speak out of turn here, but—in the immortal words of Sylvester Stallone in *Rocky 5* (or *Rocky 6* or *Rocky 117,* I can't recall), after ten years of marriage, we "still have a little something left in the basement," if you know what I mean.*

---

*And if you don't know what I mean, I'm not implying that we have a sex dungeon in our basement. Just that we still get it on.

And while I won't get into raw specifics about what was going on behind our slightly ajar door on this particular Friday night, let me try to set the stage.

It was around nine o'clock. I was cuddling with the kid, having just read her a bedtime story. It's a lovely ritual that brings the day to a sweet close in a warm, cozy fashion, so warm and cozy, in fact, that nine times out of ten I pass out in her bed, only to wake up sometime around one in the morning with the hardback version of *Goodnight Moon* splayed across my face and a Barbie-shaped kink in my shoulder. Most nights I stumble out of her room like some sorority girl doing the walk of shame out of a neighboring frat house. Other nights the husband will rouse me and send me to our bed at a decent hour, sparing me permanent damage to my face and back.

On this particular night I awoke to him giving me a gentle shake/shove. When I staggered dead-eyed into the bedroom, he gave me a come-hither glance and whispered sweet nothings to me: "WANNA DO SOME (*euphemism for intercourse*)-ING?"

It was no wonder he'd gotten turned on—I was wearing my third-most-flattering yoga pants and a T-shirt/sports-bra combo that squishes my breasts together into one long, ready-for-anything uniboob.

I shook the cobwebs from my head like a Looney Tunes cartoon character, and then responded to his offer by purring something seductive like, "Y'ARIGHT, LET'S GO."

We commenced our foreplay routine. On that night we decided to go with #4A, though we did shake it up with a few added elements—and again, I won't go into too much detail so as not to embarrass you, dear reader.* But I will say that I did reach into my bedside table in which we have a small selection of, let's just call them "implements," that were given to me as jokey shower gifts back when we got married. While the rubber on the majority of them has turned to sticky dust, and while the thing that works on AAA batteries is now corroded (though there was that time it turned itself on spontaneously in the middle of the day), there is one device that does still work, and therefore is put into service on occasion, and yes, this was one of those occasions that we plugged it in and let it work its magic.

Fast-forward, maybe twelve minutes or so—again, I won't go into much detail here, though I will say that my thigh muscles were being worked to capacity and that I was making good use of my balancing skills, while the husband was exercising his neck muscles and his ability to hyperextend his elbows. Also, three of our most supportive pillows were in use.

Imagine what you will (and feel free to reference the author's photo on the back cover, though, full disclosure, my hair was considerably less coiffed by this point), just know that things were progressing and going fairly well— I'm guessing somewhere around a "B+" if we were being graded—and we were both poised to "complete our tasks," you might say, when I happened to turn my head

---

*Particularly if dear reader is my husband. Or my in-laws.

and see the child standing at the bedroom door, rubbing her sleepy eyes.

"MOMMA?"

The husband and I froze for a split second, before un-coupling with the force of a gasoline explosion. One moment we were on the bed, and the next we were separated by the approximate length of a football field. The husband somersaulted into a pile of laundry only to emerge fully clothed, wrapped in a pillowcase, my yoga pants, and a "Got Milk?" baseball cap, while I stood there, nude (except for socks; it was November in Chicago—don't judge), babbling incoherently ("Hi hah huh, why are you, do you need pee, or glass water, you need, Mommy's cold, I'm just going to put this dish towel around my legs"), and wondering if we had just scarred our child for life.*

Without warning, the kid emitted a gleeful shriek, ran to the bed, climbed up onto it, and began jumping.

"BOUNCE TIME!" she squealed. "BOUNCE TIME!"

Clearly, she was very *not* disturbed by what she had seen—if anything, she was in a state of pure delight, having gleaned that we were in the middle of some hilariously bouncy party game—and she wanted in on the fun too.

It took some delicate wrangling—underscored by my saying no in every tone imaginable—but I was finally able to usher the child back into her own room for the night.

The husband and I crawled back into our bed. He switched off the light, and we both went to sleep, because

---

*As I had been when I was a child (please see Chapter 4).

by that point we were both too tired, too disturbed, and frankly in denial of our sexual organs to even consider resuming our previously scheduled activities.

Several nights later, now mostly healed from the shell shock and mortification, the husband and I endeavored to finish what we had started. This time we closed the door and were taking a no-nonsense, no-acrobatics, almost surgical approach to the finish line— when I heard a slow CLICK, looked up and again saw the kid standing in the doorway. This time she was holding an armful of dolls and giggling in that high creepy voice that, in movies, usually signals the arrival of the Antichrist.

It was even more shocking the second time around—it was as though she had developed some sort of perv-y sixth sense that, coupled with her then four-year-old fighting weight (which meant she was not quite heavy enough to make the floors creak), allowed her to simply materialize like the sex-murdering specter that she was.

One week later we installed a lock on the door. It seemed a perfect solution, and it was, in that it effectively kept her out of eyeball's reach. But it also prompted her to sit outside our door and wail—and FYI, it is darn near impossible to achieve any sense of "closure" when someone is pounding their tiny fists on your bedroom door and yelling, "NO BOUNCE! NO BOUNCE!"

Concerned that, were we to allow this *coitus interruptus unbefuckinglievabus* to continue, the husband would suffer from permanent blue ballage, we decided that the time had come for a conversation about boundaries and privacy. I would take the lead, and he would stand by to add color commentary on an as-needed basis.

We planned to keep it simple and unemotional, and just like the parenting books tell you to do when embarking on a sensitive conversation, we would answer her questions but wouldn't go into any more detail than necessary.

I unlatched the door and picked up the teary-eyed little party crasher.

"I WANNA BOUNCE ON YOUR BED."

"It's nighttime. Everyone is going to sleep."

I carried her into her room and tucked her in. The husband stood at the doorway while I sat on the edge of the bed and started. "When Mommy and Daddy's bedroom door is closed, that means they are having special time together and they need their privacy."

"BUT THAT MAKES ME SAD." Her lower lip folded into a floppy pout.

"I know. But part of being a big girl is understanding that sometimes people need their privacy."

She stuck her thumb in her mouth and was quiet for a moment. Then:

"MOMMA?"

"Yes?"

"WHY DO YOU PUT THAT LONG THING IN YOUR BUM?"

Now it was my turn to be quiet for a moment.

"What?"

"THAT LONG THING IN YOUR PURSE THAT FELL OUT AT THE BANK."

I quickly ascertained that she was referring to a tampon; those things leap out of my purse in public on a biweekly basis. (The husband clearly had not yet ascertained what she was referring to, as he was staring at me from the doorway, mouthing the words, "WHAT THE FUHHH?!")

"That's called a tampon. And I don't put it in my bum."

Thumb in mouth. Another pause.

"MOMMA?"

"Yes?"

"WHAT IS A SPECIAL HUG?"

Er. That was not a phrase she'd heard from us.

"Where did you hear that?"

"I DUNNO. I JUST KNOW IT."

Sure you do. "Did Rebecca tell you that word?"

She shrugged and stuck her thumb back in her mouth, then pulled it out to ask:

"IS THE LONG THING FOR WHEN YOU'RE SPECIAL HUGGING?"

"Let's get back to the first thing we were talking about. Did you understand what I said about privacy?"

She shrugged, stuck her thumb in her mouth, and stared at me.

This was not going as I'd hoped. We were entering I'm-not-even-close-to-being-ready-for-this-talk territory.

I looked to the husband for moral support. I couldn't see his face, as it was in his hands. All I could see were his shoulders, quaking. He was either laughing hysterically or crying uncontrollably, either of which would have been understandable—but totally unacceptable—in that moment.

Then I had a brainstorm—a flash of a tactic that had worked for us in the past. Songs! She responded very well to music. When washing her hands caused her to wail as though they were being dipped in battery acid, I came up with the "Hands Washing Song." When potty training was going so slowly it seemed she would be wearing Cinderella diapers at her wedding, I improvised the "Peepee on the Potty Song."

Example:

> *Today I made a pee-pee on the potteeee*
> *Today I made a pee-pee on the potteeee*
> *Today I made a pee-pee on the potteeee*
> *And now I get a stick-er! Bing Bong!*

(I never said I was Elton John—my point is that my songs did the trick.)

"I have an idea," I said. "Let's sing the 'Privacy Song.'"

"WHAT'S THAT?"

I improvised a jaunty little tune—and I don't mean to brag, but improvising songs for four-year-olds in the middle of the night, this is where I really shine.

> *It's the privacy song!*
> *It's the privacy song!*
> *Asking for privacy is never wrong*
> *It's the pri-va-cy sooooong!*

We sang it a few times until I was sure she had it.

"So what does it mean when Mommy and Daddy's door is closed?"

"PRIVACY," she said.

"Right. Any more questions?"

She shook her head, gave me a sleepy smile, then stuck her thumb in her mouth and rolled over.

And I must say, feeling awash with pride as I was, I may have strutted out of her bedroom—and yes, as I passed the husband, I may have even leaned in for a high-five. I didn't get the high-five return—but the spirit of celebration was with us approximately twenty minutes later when we climbed back in the saddle, finally closing the deal that we had embarked upon, lo, those many days ago.

We were both rounding the corner to home plate when we heard the unmistakable sound of our doorknob being rattled. We both paused and waited for the rattling to stop—which it did, only to be followed by another sound, that of a tiny voice whispering outside the door:

"YOU'RE HAVING PRIVACY."

And then, as I suppose I really should have predicted, the little specter laid down, pressed her lips up to the crack between the floor and our door, and proceeded to serenade us:

> *IT'S THE PRIVACY SONG,*
> *IT'S THE PRIVACY SONG,*
> *IT'S THE PRIVACY SONG . . .*

twenty-two

THE FIRST EMERGENCY ROOM VISIT

We are at a children's birthday party at the neighborhood community center, watching eighteen sugar-fueled preschoolers chase soccer balls around a brick-walled gym.

My husband and I are standing at the sidelines of this hilariously clumsy spectacle, gorging ourselves on tiny boxes of cranberry juice and postage-stamp-size cold pizza, and placing bets on which one of the kids will be the next to fall down. (I realize that may sound twisted, but we've logged enough afternoons at these big group birthday-party snooze fests that we've learned to create our own entertainment.)

I sprinkle a package of parmesan cheese into my mouth and then whisper to my husband, "How long before one of those uncoordinated four-year-olds takes a header into the brick wall?" And just as this thought is crossing my cheese-slowed synapses and finding its way out of my cranberry juice–stained mouth . . . our uncoordinated four-year-old takes a header into the brick wall.

Let me just say this: I'm a huge fan of physical comedy, so it's not entirely my fault that when she bounced off the wall, I almost laughed out loud.[*] [†] Of course when I saw the red stuff coming out of her head, the laugh urge disappeared entirely and was replaced by horror, guilt, and fear.

The husband—the guy I usually tease for being an outrageous overreactor[‡]—is in this instance reacting entirely appropriately, because before I can even register the fact that she has, in fact, run face-first into a jagged piece of metal hanging off the window frame, he has sprinted to her and is cradling her in his arms.[§]

I sprint toward them, praying to every god I've ever heard of, God, Jesus, Jehovah, Allah, Vishnu, Zeus: Please, please, let it not be terrible. Please, please, please, don't let this be that moment, the moment that everything changes. I'll stop being a clueless asshole, I swear to every single one of you.

---

[*] Okay, I did laugh out loud.

[†] I think we can all agree that the blame lies squarely at the feet of the Three Stooges, Carol Burnett, Jim Carrey, and Mr. Bean.

[‡] As per Exhibit C of "The Marriage Quotient," p. 115.

[§] Necessary spoiler alert: she's fine. But judging by the blood that was gushing/pouring from her at the time, it seemed that she would not be. Now back to the unspoiled remainder of the story.

The husband—whose shirt is now spattered with her blood—holds our whimpering daughter in his arms, and we both get a good look at the wound.

It's a small cut on her forehead, just above the eyebrow. Thankfully, it isn't terrible—it seems that this day will not be one of "those" days. We have been spared a life-changing catastrophe. Thanks, gods, I owe every single one of you, and henceforth will stop being a clueless asshole.[*]

Another parent hands us some napkins to help clean up the blood, as well as wipe away the child's tears, which are subsiding. Now that the initial shock has worn off, I take another look at the wound.

Here is where I need to tell you that when I was in college I was planning to be a doctor. I had taken all of my pre-med requirements in college, and becoming an MD was pretty much my fallback plan right up until the point that I decided to take the much more lucrative and practical route of becoming a professional mime.[†] Regardless, as a barely trained almost-doctor, this minor medical emergency is pretty much in my wheelhouse.

Analyzing the wound with what little knowledge I can recall from Intro to Basic Human Biology, Course #3825, I note that it appears to be quite deep. The kind of deep where you are suddenly reminded that humans are not so different from chickens, at least when it comes down to what our meat looks like underneath our skin. When the cut does not stop bleeding, the husband suggests that

---

[*] To the absolute best of my ability, I swear.

[†] Honestly, it really did seem like a good idea at the time.

we take her to the hospital because she may need stitches. Yup. Couldn't agree more. He suggests I pull the car around so that he can carry her out. Again, capital idea. I grab my keys and take a step for the door—or, rather, I tell my leg to take a step, but it defies my instructions, deciding that, thanks anyway, but it would prefer to buckle and lay down on the floor instead. And then the other leg joins its sister in quiet solidarity.

The husband looks down at me. "You okay?"

I look up at him from the floor. "Me? Yes, I'm fine. I'm going to get the car now." I try to stand, but this time it's my eyeballs that aren't up for cooperating—apparently, they have plans to cross and meet somewhere over my nose.

"I might just need a minute," I say.

The mother of the birthday boy asks how she can help—she's upset and feels terrible about what has happened, so I try my best to appear calm and collected, as though laying cross-eyed on the cigarette-burned carpeted floor of a Chicago community center is the way in which a calm and collected almost-doctor reacts in a medical emergency.

She takes my keys and leaves to get the car, while the husband focuses on holding the bloody child, and I focus on holding the swirling cranberry juice and pizza in my stomach.

⤳

The husband drives while I (still unable to conjure a vertical position) lay in the back next to the kid in her car seat. Determined to be at least the tiniest bit helpful, I strain to hold a bunch of balled-up napkins to my daughter's forehead while she happily eats her cake and bleeds.

Laying there in the backseat, watching the tops of the trees as they fly past the car window, I am dumbfounded. Not only did I once intend to become a doctor, but I have always prided myself on my ability to remain calm in crisis. I once dated a guy who nicknamed me "Clutch" for just that reason. Sure, he was a Civil War reenactor who thought he was psychic and could channel fallen Union soldiers—but still, even he could see that I was brave, strong, and dependable. How will I achieve my fantasy of a late-in-life career change and become a doctor at age sixty-three if this is how I react to a little flesh wound?

We enter the emergency room area, my daughter now covered in blood, cake, and icing, but otherwise in pretty good spirits. Her dad thinks this is a great time to tease me and asks if I need a wheelchair. Ha ha ha.

One wheelchair later, we roll into the examination room.

A nurse comes in and asks my daughter to lie down on the examination table so she can prep her for stitches. At the mere mention of the word *stitches,* I feel the pull of my eyes crossing, so I lie down right next to the kid. The kid laughs. "MAMA, WHY ARE YOU LYING DOWN? YOU'RE NOT GETTING STITCHES." I tell my unflappable little girl that I just want to be near her and leave out the part about me being a flappably flappy, almost-fainting mess.

In walks the on-duty doctor, and even from my nauseous, sideways vantage point, I can see how attractive he is, like he's just stepped off the set of *That Show With All*

The Hot Doctors. I'm almost outraged at how good-looking he is, with his perfect dreadlocks and perfect skin and perfect teeth that are so perfectly aligned and bright when he smiles I swear to God I can hear them sparkle. I look over at the four-year-old—she is enthralled; apparently, she can hear his teeth sparkle too. I glance at the husband; there's no mistaking his reaction—he too is agog, mouth hanging just a tiny bit open.* †

Dr. Perfect pulls a chair up to the examination table. "So I heard there's a soccer star in here. Which one of you is it?" The kid giggles and tells him, "ME. I EVEN SCORED A GOAL!"

"That's awesome. Fist pound!" They exchange a bonding fist-pound explosion, and then he leans over to give her forehead a close look. "Wait a minute . . . It looks like . . . Why is there icing all over your face? Are you so sweet that you have icing in your blood?" She giggles some more. This guy is good. If he really is on a TV show—and I don't see how he can't be—I am going to have to start recording it immediately.

The husband comes over to watch as the doctor examines the cut, manipulating it, causing it to open and close like a tiny, toothless mouth. I want to be strong, but every time that cut opens, I want to crawl up inside my own birth canal.

---

*In all fairness, this is a point of contention: the husband claims he was simply taken aback by how young the doctor appeared to be; I say there's no shame in a heterosexual male having his breath taken away by a perfect specimen of manhood. Who's to say who's right?

†I am.

Doctor Sparkleteeth turns to me lying on the table and gives me a sympathetic look. "How are you doing? You okay?"

"Me?" I squeak. "I'm good." Then a nurse wheels a table of instruments over and holds up an anesthetic-filled needle. I close my eyes and blow a small stream of air through my mouth, just like I learned during that birthing class I took back in '06.

After he administers the anesthetic and while he is waiting for it to take effect, Dr. Wonderful looks at me with understanding (and possibly just the tiniest bit of desire—though I suppose it's possible I was reading into it).

"You're doing great, Mom."

"I bet you see a lot of freaked-out parents come through here," I say.

"Yeah," he says. "But you gotta keep in mind, when a child gets an injury like this, there's a serious risk of secondary injury, to the heart . . . "

"Wait—what? . . .!"

"The *parent's* heart." he says, his eyes boring into mine.

Now if I'd read that in a book, I probably would have gagged. But hearing it from his full lips, I just want to bawl my eyes out in gratitude.

"Give yourself a break," he says. "Seeing your child in pain is one of the most upsetting and stressful events a parent can go through." Then he leans in even closer and whispers, his minty-fresh breath like a cool breeze in my ear, "We once had an off-duty surgeon come through here. Fainted when he saw his son's dislocated shoulder."

I don't know if it's just a line, but I really don't care. If I learned just one thing during my time as a never-will-be-doctor, it's that if it works, a placebo is just as good as the real thing.

As Dr. Smooooooth stitches up the kid, she doesn't even cry. She just keeps on talking about soccer, birthday parties, princesses, and all of the other things that transfix a four-year-old as she gazes into the eyes of her hero.

And whether it's his bedside manner, his deep-brown eyes, the way he fills out his scrubs—or the fact that he has healed my wounds, too—I too make it through her stitches without fainting, crying, or vomiting. I'm even able to sit up when it comes time to say good-bye to young Dr. Mm-mm-mmm as he leaves to return to the set of *That Show With All The Hot Doctors,* or wherever it is that abnormally handsome young physicians go after repairing the tiny bodies of their patients and their parents' troubled hearts.

twenty-three

LIES I HAVE TOLD MY DAUGHTER

Mommy and Daddy were just hugging • I don't know what happened to the rest of your cake. Maybe you ate it in your sleep? • That's exactly how much Halloween candy you came home with last night. It just looks like less to you because your eyeballs grew larger overnight • Mommy was just helping Daddy find something that he dropped in his pants; now go to your room • No, Mommy has never smoked a cigarette • If you don't brush your hair, the Haircut Fairy might come in the middle of the night, and in the morning you'll wake up bald • Yes, every other three-year-old in the city knows how to wipe her bum by herself • No, Mommy has never tried drugs • That's not zucchini; those are long, skinny apples • Isabella is wrong—hamburgers are not made from nice animals with long eyelashes • You hate soda. Remember that time you tried it and it made you cry? • No, Mommy has never been in trouble with the police • You misheard Grandpa—he was talking about "plucking" • I'm so sorry, but they just made gum chewing illegal in this county • I have no idea how your toy drum with the squeaky, southern singing voice that always sounds like she's auditioning for a Nashville record producer wound up in the garbage, smashed into tiny pieces. That *is* weird • We can't go to Disneyland—it's closed this year • No, Mommy has never set a house on fire • This is not bubble gum; it's special chewing medicine the dentist gave me for my mouth • Daddy's lying. Mommy was never a professional mime • Yes, Zippy does look different. That must be why he was resting yesterday—he was saving his energy for a growth spurt and so he could change the colors of his fins • Mommy was choking, and so Daddy was giving Mommy something called the "Heimlich maneuver," and no, we weren't naked; we were just wearing invisible clothes. Now go back to sleep.

twenty-four

THE UNDYING TRUTH

We are spending a perfect day at the park.

The daughter is in the sandbox, playing with a little boy named Giacomo while his mother sits on a nearby bench. Though we are the only two adults here, the mother and I are not friends, nor are we engaged in idle-playground new-mom chitchat. That's because she speaks no English, and I speak no Italian; as I said, it's a *perfect* day. (I have always felt—and hated—the pressure to start a friendship with another mother based solely on the fact that we both had unsafe intercourse with our respective spouses in roughly the same twelve-month time span. Sorry, ladies— simultaneous bonking does not a BFF make.)

Giacomo, however, *does* speak English, and I am enjoying the sounds of his adorable, four-year-old

Italian-waiter accent as he and my kid chat their way through random topics, every one of them a passionate non sequitur.

Giacomo: "THE SUN, EEEEEET IS SO YELLLLLOW AND RRRROUND!"

My Kid: "I HAVE PINK SANDALS!"

Giacomo: "I AM VERRRRRY GOOOOD AT SWEEMMING!"

My Kid: "MY UNCLE IAN IS ALLERGIC TO PEANUTS!"

Giacomo: "DOOO YOOOOU LIIIEEEKE DOGS-AH?!"

My Kid: "I SAW A FAIRY ONCE!"

Then Giacomo lobs, "MY PAPA, 'E IS A DOCTOR-RR-EH, BUT TODAY 'E IS A LEEEETTLE BEET SICK."

My daughter asks why is he sick. Did he eat too much candy? (Yes, that is one of the lies that I tell her. It's just my attempt to save her from my own sick Skittles dependency from which I suffer on an hourly basis.)

Giacomo says, "EH, NO. HE HAS DE FLU AND 'E WILL BE BETTERRRR, MAYBE TOMORROW. BUT ONE DAY 'E WEEEEELL BE DEAD."

My daughter, clearly alarmed by this nuclear bomb of information, half says/half questions, "HE'S NOT GO-ING TO DIE? . . ."

Giacomo says with a cheerful smile, "EH, YES, ONE DAY HE WILL DIE. AND SO TOO WEEEEELL YOUR MOTHERRR."

My daughter looks at Giacomo like he has just slapped her across the cheek with a full-grown halibut. And then she proceeds to cry her fish-slapped face off.

I look to Giacomo's mom, who, native language not-withstanding, doesn't seem as alarmed as she really ought to be, considering that her son has clearly just shoved my daughter into an emotional abyss.

Giacomo turns and says something to her in Italian ("BLA BLA BLA BLA MOR-TAY"), his chubby little sand-covered hands gesturing cartoonishly. His mother listens, then shrugs and nods at me as if to say, "Eh, yes, someday you too will be dead, eh?" *

Then Giacomo nods and says one more time (because once wasn't enough), "YES, YOUR MOTHERRRR, ONE DAY-EE SHE WEEELL BE DEAD." He then shrugs his little shoulders and returns to building a sand castle, or perhaps it was a sand mortuary, I don't recall.

Thanks, Giacomo, you little mini-sadist. I was hoping to address this issue a whole lot later, maybe over some floating Sea Monkeys, but I guess now is as good a time as any.

I take my little blonde wailing mess into my chest, wrap my arms around her, and utter some long "sssshhhh" sounds that I believe to be reassuring. She pulls away, looks me straight in the eyes, and asks between sobs, "IS IT TRUE, MOMMY? ARE YOU GOING TO DIE?"

---

*Look. I know that writing about my own death is foolhardy at the worst, and just plain bad form at best. Not only am I "courting" the devil; I'm also courting the devil's children, i.e., Internet jagoffs, those delightful vermin. I can hear the online comments now, "Thank GOD she's ded! Good riddince to that Moe-ron! She can suk it!—Sincerely, livinginmy-momsbasement@aol.com." On the other hand, I believe firmly in mentally tracking a horrible idea to its logical, horrible conclusion, thereby guaranteeing that it NEVER HAPPENS. And so, by this reasoning I have just guaranteed myself immortality. That's science.

Now I am sure there's a right way to answer this question, but I am also sure that I couldn't find the answer, not even if I had a million monkeys Googling on a million laptops for a period of eight to ten weeks.

It occurs to me that I could just lie and say, "Of course not, silly! That's never going to happen!" But I won't lie.[*] When it comes to my kid, I believe in total honesty, mainly because I have the memory of a thumbtack, and keeping track of lies is a practical impossibility for me; also because I fear the sick and ironic sense of humor of an entity/being/god-thingy who would strike me down instantly for telling such a whopper.

But I'm also unsure how to tell this particular truth. I come from a long line of emotional avoiders, especially where death is involved. I am obsessed with it.[†]

And while other women like to visualize their weddings or map out their fantasy European vacations, I like to plan my own funeral.[‡] [§]

"IS IT TRUE, MOMMY?"

---

[*]About big stuff. Little stuff—well, please see previous chapter.

[†]As is reflected in Chapter 10 ("My Bodies, Myself"), a true story, BTW, and one that I tell at the drop of a hat, so be sure to invite me to your next cocktail gathering. Or you could just reread that chapter. But invite me to your cocktail party anyway.

[‡]I want to be dressed in my flesh-colored Lycra bodysuit, the one with the fake nipples and pubic hair attached (you'll find it with all my other sewing stuff). I want a big jazz band, the kind they have in New Orleans. And a parade. Also, I want my friends, the ones who have stopped talking to each other—and whose feud makes brunch planning particularly difficult—to be forced to hug. For an excruciatingly long time. Also, there should be pie.

[§]This may be moot, as I believe I've already established my intention to remain immortal.

On the other hand—and this is a big, wart-covered hand—I am unmatched in my ability to believe that I and my loved ones are all immortal (despite the fact that none of us are vampires—not proven, anyway). Like the majority of idiots in our blissfully dopey North American culture, I have done a very good job, thank-you-very-much, of living in total avoidance of death.

Point of fact: A few years ago, just a few months after the death of my great-aunt Naomi (one of the craziest, loudest, most foul-mouthed, and wonderful old bats you could ever hope to meet), I was on the phone with my dad when he said, "I was talking to your brother the other day. He didn't know that Naomi had died. Isn't that weird?" I wanted to say, "No, Dad, that's not weird. What's weird is the fact that none of us thought to call and tell him that she'd died. *That's* what's weird—the fact that our entire freaking family is in denial of our mortality!" Instead, I said, "Yeah, Dad. That is weird."

"*IS IT TRUE, MOMMY?*"

I am experiencing complete mental paralysis; give me the existence of God . . . How gravity works . . . Bestiality even. I'll explain them all a thousand ways and with pictures. Just please, not this one.

"*IS IT TRUE?*"

This moment is going to take delicacy and tact. And sensitivity. So I look her straight in the eyes, and with all the sincerity I can muster I say, "Hey, are you hungry for ice cream, cuz I sure am!!"

But no, the child is not hungry for ice cream. Not for the first time since ever.

As my mind races to find new evasion tactics, the kid stops crying and looks at me with a fake smile on her face and an odd sense of calm. She asks again, "IS IT TRUE, MOMMY? ARE YOU GOING TO DIE?"

With every iota of energy in my body, I fight the urge to avoid, deflect, joke, or subject-change. Instead, I take a deep breath and say, "One day, a very, very, very, very, very, very long time from now . . . *yes*."

I start to back that up with some Lion King "circle of life" rhetoric, how "if nothing ever died, then there would be no room for anything else to grow . . . ," but I have lost her. If the earlier tears were a storm, she is now at a Category 5 Typhoon. And yet as unmoored as this makes me feel, there is a tiny part of me that is watching her and marveling at the depth of her sadness. Here I am, decades older than this kid, and I have never in my life felt this kind of grief (because, as I mentioned, I come from a family of emotional moe-rons).

Unbelievably, some mothering instinct in me kicks in. I hold her and rock her and say over and over how it's not going to happen for a long time, then touch every wooden surface we pass as I carry her (all forty-nine pounds of her) four blocks home.

She calms down enough that her wailing becomes a whimper. I bring her into the house where we find her dad. He can see from her tear-stained, poppy-red face that something emotionally gnarly has gone down. This is confirmed when she flings herself into his chest and then looks into his face and says, "I'm really going to miss Mommy."

He gives me a "What the fo?" look, and it takes me a moment but finally I understand what is going on in that troubled head of hers: she has taken Giacomo at his word. "One day, your mother will die." According to my four-year-old, death isn't a universal concept to be grasped, absorbed, and wrestled with for a lifetime. It's a selective piece of bad news and apparently applies to only me. (And maybe Giacomo's dad.)

As her tears subside, I decide to let her misunderstanding lie, at least for the moment. We've had enough trauma for one afternoon, and I don't have the heart to correct her misinterpretation by informing her that one day not only will I die, but so will her dad, and her grandparents, and her dog, her fish, her roly-polies in the garden, and her friends.

And so, too, will she.

And now it's not just for her sake that I hold back this unwieldy truth. Because as that singular thought leaps across my taxed synapses, emotional ignoramus that I may be, I start to cry too. And so as her confounded dad watches in utter confusion, I allow my frustration with small, socially advanced Italian children to fall by the wayside, and I hug her and stroke her hair and pray to the ironic being in the sky for as many sandbox days as she or he sees fit to give us, wood touches or not.

twenty-five

THE BEGINNING OF THE END

The Road to Parenthood is littered with tired clichés that crawl up my rectum, fuse my spine, and embarrass me on behalf of normal-brained humans everywhere.

"Cherish every moment."

This out-of-touch phrase is often uttered by the type of person who, when you dated them back in college, insisted on saving every birthday card, restaurant receipt, movie ticket, and used condom.

"You'll never know love until you have a child."

This speaker achieves the impressive feat of offending (a) anyone who doesn't have a child and (b) all of the other people in his or her life that aren't his or her child.

"Parenthood is the toughest job you'll ever love."

This saying has actually been co-opted from the Peace Corps, so unless you're quoting this line while tilling a rice paddy in Myanmar, you'd best be advised to shut your First World trap.

"Enjoy it. It goes so fast."

This is the in-bred granddaddy of all parenting clichés, the one that fails to acknowledge all those painfully tedious moments of parenthood in which time is not speeding but dragging like a garden slug that has just slithered through a puddle of tequila-infused molasses.

Like sitting with your child as she takes ten minutes to sound out "Thhhhhhaaaat ffffffffaaaaaaaaaat rrrrrrr-raaaaaaaaat sssssssssaaaaaaaat ooooooooooooooonnnn-nnn thhhhhhhhhhhhhhe mmmmmmmaaaaaaaaaat . . . " (which, while an important part of a strong educational foundation, is also recognized by the CIA as a legitimate alternative to waterboarding). Or when your kid begs you to press play on her *Nursery Rhymes Set to '80s Death Metal!* CD over and over and over and over until you start wondering what it would feel like to ram your car into the side of that building right there. Or when your kid is having trouble putting on her G.D. shoes but refuses to let you help her even though you're already forty-five minutes late for a playdate at the park where the first thing she's going to do is take off her G.D. shoes. Or when your kid loses/breaks/destroys something of yours that is special and irreplaceable.*

Bottom line is, being a parent is not all sunshine and lollipops. Sometimes it's sun damage and diabetes.

⇜

It's the first day of kindergarten. While the other parents assembled in this tiny classroom are struggling to cover their tears, I'm fighting to hide my glee.

The past five years—watching that squirming, screaming little squid blossom into a fully formed human—have been an amazing ride. But I'd be lying if I said that I haven't been eagerly awaiting this day and this new chapter, this chance to watch her slowly gain independence as I greedily take back some of my own.

No longer must I fake the stomach flu just to get a precious few minutes in the bathroom alone . . . No more will I have to argue over who gets to walk the dog ("It's my turn! Give me that friggin leash!"), or fight over whose turn it is to go grocery shopping ("You're damn right I'm going to the store right now. We're out of Herbes de Provence!"). Deep down in my soul lives a tiny Mel Gibson, his weird face covered in blue, his cries of "FREEEEEDOOOOM!" echoing in my head.

---

*Like those fake buckteeth with braces that fitted you so perfectly and that you wore the first time you met your husband's high school friends, and for twenty incredible minutes they actually believed they were real; and then your four-year-old had to go and try them on the dog, and when you saw how they'd been obliterated and covered in dog saliva, you had to bite the inside of your cheek to keep from crying, and you've spent the last year trying to replace them, but you'll never find another pair like them, may they rest in peace.

Though he's trying hard not to show it, the husband is something of a wreck. He's always been very protective of the child, whereas I am a dedicated follower of the Cult of Benign Neglect. He still cuts her grapes into sixteenths and drenches her in sunblock with an SPF of 15,000, sunblock that is so thick, it leaves her looking like a silent-film star. Right now he is hovering over the kid and cycling through his Kindergarten Preparedness Checklist for the twentieth time today, "Do you have your hat? Are you warm enough? Do you need to pee? Where's your hand sanitizer?"

Finally, he releases her from his clutches. The kid stares nervously in the direction of the play area, then at us. Though every instinct is telling me to "LEAVE! FLEE! YOU'VE GOT SIX HOURS OF FREEDOM AND TIME'S A-WASTING!" I cool my jets and stand my ground, then dig into my purse, where I find an old napkin balled up at the bottom; I hold it at the ready to dry her tears. Then the kid fakes us out with a quick "BUH-BYE!" and disappears into a tiny pretend kitchen.

Having fulfilled my duty, I make my way (trying hard not to giggle and/or skip) through the sea of still-clinging parents. One mother is weeping and squeezing her son so tightly, it seems she's auditioning for Meryl Streep's role in the remake of *Sophie's Choice.*

Standing in the doorway is our daughter's new kindergarten teacher, who looks like she's probably a very nice lady, but at the moment her polite smile is doing very little to hide her inner monologue, which I'm guessing sounds like "Hello, nice to meet you all. Now get the hell out of my classroom, you child-suffocating messes."

I give the teacher a quick wink-nod combo, as if to say, "Can you believe these poor saps?" She gives me a look back as if to say, "You can get the hell out too," so I squeeze past her and the rest of the still-weeping/loitering throng and then notice I've lost the husband. He's back near the tiny kitchen, running through Kindergarten Preparedness Checklist #21 with the kid. Clearly, he needs a few more minutes—but me, I'm out.

I exit the classroom and head out to the empty playground, where I sit at the bottom of the slide and revel in the glory of this moment.

I've always thought of the job of being a parent as something between a Sherpa and a good party host; that my job is to guide her (Follow me up the mountain/to the hors d'oeuvres table), point out the sights (Look, an eagle!/the dance floor!), warn her of the dangers (Beware, that ledge/that guy is slippery/a douche), and to just try to show her a good time while not letting her fall off the mountain/get drunk and pass out on some weird dude's lap.

Still, I can't help feeling that it's a near miracle we've made it this far, considering the multitude of ways that things could have gone spectacularly wrong during her upbringing*—yet there she is, starting kindergarten like the normal, undamaged person that we have somehow managed to raise.

---

*Please see Chapters 1–24.

And though this moment represents just how far we've come, as I close my eyes and lay back against the smooth, sun-warmed, and vaguely pee-smelling slide, my mind wanders along the path of "firsts" that are still yet to come:

Today she'll make a best friend, a sweet little girl who is polite and shy . . . and then one day she'll have her first best-friend breakup, with that same little girl whom I've always secretly hated and thought was a sneaky and manipulative little creep.

Then will come the first sleepover away from home, where she'll stay up past midnight giggling and sneaking snacks, and where she'll discover that not all mothers stay up late squeezing their chest pimples, Googling their ex-boyfriends, and gorging on Duncan Hines frosting from the can.

Then will come middle school, makeup, shoplifting, and puberty—not necessarily in that order—and the first time she screams "IHATEYOURFRIGGINGUTS!" and really, truly means it.

Then the first time she asks to borrow the car, though by then it'll be some sort of teleportation device that runs on renewable resources of squirrel urine and Starbucks coffee-cup sleeves.

Then will come her prom and her first kiss at the front door, while I flick the patio lights on and off, yelling,

"GET IN THE HOUSE!!!" which will lead to her screaming "IHATEYOURFRIGGINGUTS!" for the second (and far from last) time.

Still deeper into our futurescape I go . . . jumping ahead a few more years to the husband and me (I've aged pretty gracefully, might I add) now dropping her off at college. It's a decent midsize school that's a bargain at a hundred thousand dollars.* She'll live in a fun, lively coed dorm where she'll have a whole bunch of first-time experiences that I hope to God I never, ever hear about.

Then we'll meet her first "serious" boyfriend. I'll think he's wonderful and will knit him four ski sweaters, only to be brokenhearted when they have a friendly breakup two weeks later. Six months down the line I'll meet Number 2; this time I'll try to keep my distance but will find myself growing fond of this kid who brings me flowers and calls me "Mrs. C." Him I'll only knit two sweaters, but again it won't work out, and again I'll take the breakup hardest of all.

Then somewhere around Number 15, this one will stick (good thing, because otherwise I might have made good on my threat to shackle him to me). He's a good person who loves her and tolerates her weird parents, and after a respectable amount of time we'll

---

*Per semester.

throw them a big, overpriced wedding at some exotic destination—like Hawaii, or maybe Jupiter, especially if they're offering group discounts.

Deeper still I go, further into the future . . .

Now we're with the daughter and the son-in-law and their children—our grandchildren: two boys and one manly little girl who call us "Paw-Paw" and "Mee-Maw," and they'll adore us, though the littlest one will be afraid to hug me because of the steel-belted-strength whisker that grows out of the mole on my chin, but I'll win her over when I show her how I can make it dance.

I'll love those children so deeply it'll be a challenge not to squeeze them until their eyes pop out. They'll grow to be good kids who share just enough of our good qualities and none of the bad ones—though the grand-daughter will test her mom/the daughter in ways that will amuse me to no end.*

And then one day I'll awaken to see their faces—all of them—at my bedside, looking down at me with love, telling me, "Go to the light, Grandma . . . Go to the light!"

And as their soft, loving voices echo in my ears, I close my eyes and rise into that big bright light, and all sound fades away and I become one with the cosmos

---

*As per Appendix B, for example.

and am filled with a sense of wonder and love and ful-
fillment and so many beautiful feelings and I am just
a vapor now or maybe a liquid or a cosmic plasma,
I'm not sure what happens at that altitude . . .

And then the fantasy melts away, and I am back on the playground. My eyes are wide open, staring at the bright-blue sky, and gushing like the falls of Niagara.

I am not ready for the light.

I am not ready for this day.

I am not ready for her to grow up and out and away from me.

My head is a mess of feelings and images and emotions and impressions—it's like someone threw a tantrum at a gift shop and dumped the Hallmark-card rack to the floor, scattering the sappy feelings all over the place.

Now I am full-on ugly crying. My vision is blurry, my face hot with tears. I wipe the tears away, but no matter how hard I rub, one of my eyes will not clear. I'm blind . . . Dear, God, I've cried so hard, I've broken my eye . . . MY EYE!!

A hand grabs my shoulder—it's the husband. He holds me as I sob, stroking my hair and whispering, "It's okay. She has her sunblock." And he pats my leg, which is where he finds the contact lens that I've simply cried out and is stuck to my jeans.

Turns out I'm not blind. I'm just another weepy parent.

I grab the balled-up napkin from the bottom of my purse and dry my soaking-wet face. My husband gives me a hug and a smile and then gently informs me that I have a candy wrapper stuck to my cheek.

On the way home we walk past our daughter's new classroom. I peek through the window and see her sitting on the carpet, listening as her teacher teaches them the "Good Morning" song.

The child's face is so vulnerable and eager, her expression one of total openness. Then her eyes shift as she notices me there. She gives me a wave and a nervous smile. It's then that I remember that she's still got a ways to go.

And, apparently, so do I.

APPENDIX A

I AM MY FATHER'S SON

Cue the sappy music and a cheap, watery fade-to-flash-back effect.

October 10, 1985. It's the night of my eighteenth birthday. Eighteen, the age at which one may become legally hammered in the city of Winnipeg, Manitoba.

My best friend, Deb, and I are standing outside the Palomino (a local bar famous for having the only working mechanical bull in western Canada), and I am dressed for eighties-style action: skin-tight black angora sweater dress, red leather stiletto shoes, and a wide red belt that hangs from my hips and converges at my groinial region in a not-so-subtle V. My hair is permed, feathered, and teased in a gravity-bashing style to which several cans of mousse have given their lives, and I am holding a burgundy pleather clutch purse that is filled with the finest drugstore cosmetics that money can buy.

This, I think, will be a night to remember, but not because I plan on joining the ranks of the hammered. Like most people who grew up on the prairies, I was getting blitzed on wine coolers in seventh grade, so the idea of spending this night getting drunk isn't especially appealing (also, I don't want to risk getting vomit on the angora—it's very hard to clean). No, this night is not about alcohol. It is about me and womanhood, and the public intersection of the two. Because while I was not born with testicles, or a tiny penis that some shaky-handed doctor accidentally exploded and then hastily converted into a makeshift vagina during a circumcision-gone-wrong; even though I was born a human girl-child with shockingly average female genitalia, I was raised as a boy.

Perhaps it was because my parents were pot-smoking, antiestablishment types who didn't believe in "gender," or maybe it was simply that after seven years of raising sons, by the time I showed up, they decided, "Screw it. Let's just stick with what we know." Whatever their reasons, it was clear my parents had no intention of indulging my second X chromosome.

If this were an audiovisual presentation, I would take you through the following slide show of my boyhood:

- There I am at age three, wearing my brothers' hand-me-down underwear, the Y-front opening of which will confound and confuse me for years to come.

- Here's me and my dad; I'm eight. We're enjoying a daddy-daughter moment in which he is teaching me a card game he has invented. This game is based on "Go Fish," only it is called "Go Fuck Yourself." He has just asked if I have any threes, and I am smiling proudly as I reply, "No, Dad . . . Go fuck yourself."

- That's me running shirtless through the neighborhood long past what should have been allowed, and there's my mom, too busy making macramé plant hangers to notice.

- Me and my dad again. He is looking at me with an expression of confusion and disbelief; that's because I've just asked him if I can take ballet lessons. He will answer my question with his own, "Why the hell would you want to prance around in airy-fairy tights?" and will suggest that I take judo instead.

- And there I am with my brothers. Here they are dangling loogies over my head; there, jamming rancid sweat socks in my face; that's a good one— one of them is giving me an Indian rope burn, while the other farts into my screaming mouth.

- The next one is me ratting out my brothers to my dad, who is taking a hit off a joint while telling us to "piss off and work it out."

So that's the following photo and every one after that: me flailing my arms like a spastic windmill, throwing wild, ineffectual punches at my brothers' respective balls.

Based on my very unscientific polling methods (i.e., having asked most of the men I've ever slept with, dated, or married), it appears that my childhood was fairly standard by most men's experiences. Which is probably why it never occurred to me that my daily existence was different from that of anyone else I knew.

Until the day that I began to develop teeny-tiny breasts and a teeny-tiny shoplifting habit to match. For it was on that day that I strolled into Woolworths and stole a pair of magnetic earrings that I traded to another preteen thief for a freshly lifted training bra. I smuggled the lacy contraband into the house and locked myself in the bathroom, feeling like a cross-dresser as I tore off my shirt and wrapped the front-clasping garment over my mosquito-bite boobs. I don't quite know how to explain what I felt, except to say that it was a religious experience, like something out of *Joseph and the Amazing Technicolor Dreamcoat,* but if the coat was actually a 32AA Playtex bra.

And thus began my life as a girl.

From that moment I took it upon myself to learn the ways of womanhood, with a self-taught curriculum that included such lessons as "How to Wear (and Stuff) a Stolen Bra," "The Mystical Powers of Mascara," and "The Subtle Art of Getting Felt Up." Over the next few years I transcended the family plot to turn me into a boy and transformed myself from a scrappy little dude into a wily, willowy woman.

Which is what I am when I find myself on the night of my eighteenth birthday, in line at the Palomino, so drenched in femininity that no one would confuse me with the boy I once was, a boy whose only ambition in life was to pee her name in the snow (though sadly, all I ever managed to spell was "oooo").

I proudly flash my license to the Beefy Bouncer at the door and then enter the promised land. As I order a virgin daiquiri I marvel at the sight of men and women flashing smiles and cleavage at each other in an ear-splitting, eye-melting blend of music, laughter, and acid-washed clothing.

Deb and I squeeze ourselves onto the crowded dance floor, where we join our age-of-majority brethren, jerking and bobbing to the hits of Huey Lewis, Wham! and De-Barge. After an hour or so, Deb parts the sweaty waters of lumbering dancers, while I fetch our purses from the bar and follow her downstairs to the ladies' bathroom.

As Deb steps into a stall to pee, I take a spot at the mirror and begin violently flipping my hair forward and back, forward and back, prepping it for the can-full of mousse I'm about to force into it. On an upswing I notice a woman enter the bathroom, her XL frame packed into an XS tank top that reads "METALLICA: Metal Up Your Ass." I detect an unsettling expression on her face, one that I instantly recognize as drug-induced, perhaps angel dust or PCP (neither of which I really know anything about except for what I'd learned from Meredith Baxter-Birney on various after-school specials).

I don't have much time to think before Crazy-Eyes lunges toward me, grabs my burgundy pleather clutch purse off the sink, and tries to run. That purse contains my most valued possessions: my grape Bonne Bell lip gloss, my bottle of Obsession knock-off perfume, my eyelash curler, and my favorite can of styling mousse.

Instinctively, I grab the end of the clutch and . . . clutch it. Crazy-Eyes snarls and says, "Give me that purse." To which I respond, "No." To which she responds by putting one arm behind my back and the rest of me in a very tight choke hold.

I try to scream, apparently unaware that one needs a working windpipe to do that. I stomp my feet, drilling red stiletto heels into her ankles, but my attacker doesn't even flinch. Deb, hearing the frantic tap-dancing sounds I'm making on the tile floor, comes to my aid, jabbing her well-manicured fingernails into the beast's arm. No reaction. Evidently, Crazy-Eyes intends to choke the life out of me, and not even acrylic nail tips are going to stop her.

As I feel my consciousness begin to slip away, two things occur to me: one, that the lasting memory of my eighteenth birthday will be of being mugged and choked out in the basement bathroom of a honky-tonk bar; and two, that because I'm sober, I won't even have the luxury of forgetting it. And then something else occurs to me: a sense of fury and indignation that I haven't felt in years, not since my brothers wrapped a postwrestling-tournament jockstrap around my face and tied it in a knot so complex it took me twenty minutes to escape.

Suddenly, my fear and panic are replaced with white-hot rage. I wrest my left arm free and flail blindly, reaching for whatever I can grab, the first thing a hank of frizzy blonde hair. With all my strength I pull the attacker's face into view, ball my right hand into a fist, and throw the hardest punch I can muster. But unlike the countless feeble shots I'd aimed at my brothers' balls over the years, this one connects squarely with a BAM in the center of my would-be killer's face. She stumbles back, hits the wall, and goes down.

As I lean against the sink to catch my breath, the door opens. It's the Beefy Bouncer, wearing a smug smile that ranks 9.5 on the Douchebag Scale. "All right, ladies, let's break up the catfight," he drawls.

Choking back tears, I say, "She . . . jumped me and . . . tried to . . . steal my purse!" My attacker mumbles, "No, she tried to steal my purse." "That's a lie!" I croak. "She's clearly inebriated, and quite likely stoned on PCP . . . and I am a designated driver!"

The bouncer asks to see my burgundy pleather clutch purse. He opens it, pulls out the wallet, and asks, "Is this yours"? I look, and with an almost audible clang my sphincter slams shut as I reply, "No, it is not."

Because it is not.

"So which one of you is 'Crystal-Anne Shymkiw'?" he asks, though the answer is fairly obvious: it's the Metallica fan writhing on the floor, though the swollen bloody nose on her face doesn't quite match the version in her driver's license photo.

I try to convince the bouncer of the hilarious! misunderstanding! that has taken place, then chase it down with an earnest apology to Miss Shymkiw, a.k.a. the Crazy-Eyed victim, for evidently having confused *her* burgundy pleather clutch purse with *my* burgundy pleather clutch purse, still located on the upstairs bar. "Can you believe we both have such bad taste?!" I joke. But she does not laugh and finds it all so unhilarious that she insists on pressing charges against me for theft and battery. Winnipeg's Finest are summoned, statements are taken, and in a lucky turn of events the cops proclaim this the funniest call they've had all week ("like an episode of *Three's Company,* eh!"), and they convince Ms. Shymkiw to drop all charges.

It's about one in the morning when I am dropped off at my parents' house. My neck is red, my voice is hoarse, my hand is bruised and throbbing. I am ragged and shaken and most of all mortified by what has happened. I drag myself into the kitchen, where my parents are enjoying a midnight munchies snack of Fig Newtons slathered with cream cheese.* When my mom asks if I had "fun" on my birthday, I lie down on the linoleum floor, then shut my eyes and open my mouth to let the story of this night spill out.

My dad asks if the other woman was badly hurt. I tell him no, but that I'd probably have to pay to get her blood-spattered Metallica shirt dry-cleaned. He nods thoughtfully. "So, in other words, you got her good," he says, then smiles, pumps a fist in the air, and shouts, "FAR FUCKING OUT!"

And so it was. Far fucking out, that is. Sure, I'd inadvertently committed "assault with intent to rob," but

---

*Delicious, BTW.

more important I'd defended myself in a barroom brawl and made my stoned dad proud in the process. His fist pump carried more than just cream-cheesy goodness that night; it gave me a grasp on my family's attempts to make me the third son. It is also the reason I say with true pride that the day I turned eighteen was the day I became a man.

APPENDIX B

AN UNCOMFORTABLE CONVERSATION THAT MY DAUGHTER WILL HAVE WITH HER TEENAGE DAUGHTER SOMETIME IN THE FUTURISTIC FUTURE

I need you to log out right now.

Don't lie. I can tell by your head movements that you're scanning the Intelliboard embedded in your retina. Log out NOW. We need to discuss what happened while you were alone in the pod today.

"Nothing?" Perhaps you'd like to take a look at what the NanoCam recorded? Siri, please play 3D NanoCam segment stamped fourteen o'clock, Earth standard time.

Now there you are walking into the kitchen . . . oh, and who is *that*? I don't recognize your "guest,"

but I'm *sure* he's just here to "help you with your homework"—

Shhhh, keep watching. It's about to get interesting . . .

Now I don't know if you caught what you said there, so I'll pull up the captioning. "Are you as hot as I am, Steve?" And there's the part where you start taking off your exogarments—aaaaaand there you are, just as naked as you were the day we brought you home from the lab!

Why are you looking away? We were just getting to the good part, where you push him up against the iFooderator and . . . my Google in Heaven, WHAT WERE YOU THINKING?? Wait, don't answer that, I know what you were thinking, because I have the transcripts from your Telepath-o-log! "16:45 p.m., April 15, 2058: 'MOM WOULD BLOW A NANOGASKET IF SHE KNEW ABOUT THIS. HA. HA. HA.'"

I just don't understand. Is this how we raised you? To swap bodily excretions in our kitchen with an unemployed Venutian named Steve?!

Just a minute. Don't turn this on me—I am *not* being species-ist! I just don't appreciate you attempting Interlinkage with some guy whose best quality is his eighteen-inch-long prehensile tongue! And just who is this "Steve" anyway? Who are his parents? Does he even *have* parents? Or is he some orphaned hatchling of questionable origin?

How dare you?! I AM A VERY UNDERSTANDING PERSON! Wasn't I understanding when you *begged* me to get your pupils pierced, even though I predicted they would get infected—which they did, requiring *very* expensive eyeball replacement? And wasn't I understanding when you "borrowed" my Interstellar Micron Transporter, then "lost" it in a black hole? Did I complain, even though I had to ride that disgusting Quasar Shuttle to work for weeks?!

All right. I'm sorry for raising my voice. I just . . . I miss the old days when you and I would spend Saturdays taking the HyperTube down into the Mall of the Core. We'd share a plate of Chocolate-esque NutriPellets and just ThinkSpeak, for hours. And now? . . . Hand me my Endorphinizer. I think I feel moisture in my tear duct.

(long inhale, long exhale)

Are you being grounded? Uh, does a cyborg evacuate its waste materials through a pneumatic-tube chamber? Yes, you're being grounded.

First you will disconnect from the MindHive for one month.

Second, there will be no SexThink. Not even with yourself. You'll just have to research how we used to do it manually. No, it's not ideal, but you've made your REM pod; now you'll have to sleep in it.

Third, you will start dressing appropriately. That means your nipples are to be covered at all times. And if I find out that you're swapping motherboards with anybody . . . That kind of behavior is fine when you're in a Committed Partnership or Conglomerate—but until then, pardon my language, but no Starbuck'ing way.

Bottom line is, I didn't undergo cryogenic freezing—TWICE!—just so that I could be defrosted and watch you behave like some twentieth-century animal.

I just wish you would heed the words of your grandmother Johanna—a very wise and extraordinarily beautiful woman—who always used to say, "Don't be flattered if a being with male characteristics demonstrates visible excitation in its penile appendage." Of course, I may be paraphrasing, but I think you get the drift.

And by the way, don't even try asking your dad for help with this one. He's in a horrible mood as it is—he was late for the Space-Time Conveyor, and now his legs and briefcase are stuck in 1973 until tomorrow afternoon. Personally, I'd leave him alone until he can reorganize himself.

Yes, we're done. Now despite everything, I want you to know that I love you, and I will never stop loving you. And I know you're upset now, but when you're four hundred you'll look back at this and laugh. Now give my jar a kiss and turn me around so I can look out the window.

ACKNOWLEDGMENTS

This book took a lot of words. And time. And snacks. And the help of a whole bunch of people to whom I am tremendously grateful.

The insanely talented folks at Perseus Books and Da Capo Press—thank you for all your hard work, your kind words, and for being so gentle with me (especially considering this was my first time). And great gobs of humongous, emphatic thanks to my editor, Renee Sedliar, for her instincts and intellect, and for our phone calls, which were consistently the funniest, most entertaining moments of my day.

Doug Abrams, thanks for putting me up to this, and for being the wisest, most honest, and intuitive literary agent I could ever have dreamed up. And thanks also to the delightful Lara Love (who, p.s., lives up to her name).

To my writer friends and to the writing groups to which I belong, past and present: Safehouse, The Disclaimers, and to my Chicago lay-deez (I don't think we ever came up with a name; we were too busy writing and snacking to do that). Thank you for your notes, feedback, laughs, and raised eyebrows in response to many of these pieces. Thanks especially for making the solitary sport of writing not quite so lonely.

Wendy Hopkins, Renee Albert, and Rebecca (The Other Manly Lady) Corry: three of the smartest, funniest first readers a gal could have. Nobody punches up like you. Or in a more positive, loving, thoughtful way. Oh god, now I'm weeping. Moving on . . .

To Dani Klein, who suggested that I start writing about my family in the first place. This book is all your fault, and for that I am eternally grateful.

Lisa Belkin, the Honest-to-Godness Godmother to this book. Thank you for your support and encouragement and for entrusting your column space to my goofy stories. And thanks for making me cry the first time I saw my name in print.

To Alanis Morissette, for your insight and inspiration, and for telling me (in your non-pushy, Canadian way) that I was going to do this, years (seriously: years) before I knew it myself.

Suzanne Luna, for not just being a cheerleader, but for being a model of what hardworking creative kick-assery looks like. I'm still not sure how you fit seven days of living into a twenty-four-hour period; my best guess: a time machine. (I look forward to an explanation when I see you next yesterday.)

Thanks to Lindsay Howard, TV agent extraordinaire, for your continued guidance and faith over the years—I'm pretty sure our relationship has lasted longer than most Hollywood marriages.

To all the caretakers who've given me the space and time to think and write, all while keeping my kid safe, happy, and fairly clean: Jessica Dooley, Tina Rajabi, Astride Noel, Claire Kander, Telma Giron, and the wonderful staff members at JCYS, TBH, and Riverside Drive Charter School.

For their generous time and excellent advice in this alien land known as publishing: Nia Vardalos, Emmy Laybourne, Brett Paesel, Claire Zulkey, Jen Coffeen, Kara Corridan, and Rich ("What What?") Fulcher.

To Story Studio Chicago, the Writers Workspace, and the WGA (for that fantastic office space with the couch that is comfy, but not overly so).

To the writing teachers who stoked my love of words and kicked my ass as they did: Amy Friedman, Neil Besner, Mr. Carruthers, and the lovely Joanie Fridell. Thanks for your enthusiasm, your dedication, and your excellent teaching. (And if you don't like what you've seen in this book, blame it on one of the other teachers who undid all of your hard work.)

To my friends and family in Winnipeg, Chicago, Austin, Calgary, New York, L.A, and beyond . . . I am one lucky so-and-so. Thanks for your encouraging words and stimulating ideas over coffee, wine, meals, and snacks (lots and lots of snacks). Thanks for your letters, e-mails and Facebook posts (the forwards, the likes, and the shares . . . oh, the shares). There are too many of you to mention by name, but I am grateful for you all, and the next time I see you, if I suddenly lay on you a too-tight hug or a wet, sloppy kiss—you'll know why.

And to Jay Leggett and Dave (Big Dave) Marks, two fine fellas who left way too soon: you are both missed, often and very much.

To Walt, Gail, Aaron, and David Stein: even if you weren't my family, I probably would have chosen to spend my days hanging out at your house (as creepy as that would have been). Mom and Dad, I'm grateful for your excellent and insightful feedback, not just on this book but on pretty much every creative endeavor I've ever taken on. Thanks for giving me a childhood worth remembering and writing about, and for your continued help and advice now that I'm the one doing the "parenting" (even if that word sticks in your respective craws).

To my in-laws Christine and Cliff, Bob and Susan, and Paul—for your humor, your acceptance, and for giving me the single greatest score of my life. I'm not sure what I did to deserve David Gassman (maybe the result of some karmic debt I incurred sometime in the fourteenth century?) . . . In any case, thank you.

To David, my BFF with benefits, for taking care of business when I was lost in my laptop screen; for allowing me to dig deep into that big, creative brain of yours, and for taming the snakes in mine; for believing in and loving me so well through this whole process; and for making me laugh every single g.d. day. You truly are the wind beneath my flappy batwings.

And finally, to Sadie, who inspired it all. I hit the life jackpot the day I became your mom. I know everybody thinks their kid is special, but just between you and me— in your case, it's true. It's a privilege to know you, and a joy to watch you grow. I love you with all my heart (and then some). Now go clean up your room.